Richard Simpson

An Introduction to the Philosophy of Shakespeare's Sonnets

Richard Simpson

An Introduction to the Philosophy of Shakespeare's Sonnets

ISBN/EAN: 9783337063078

Printed in Europe, USA, Canada, Australia, Japan

Cover: Foto ©Thomas Meinert / pixelio.de

More available books at **www.hansebooks.com**

PHILOSOPHY

OF

SHAKESPEARE'S SONNETS.

LONDON: PRINTED BY
SPOTTISWOODE AND CO., NEW-STREET SQUARE
AND PARLIAMENT STREET

AN INTRODUCTION TO THE

PHILOSOPHY

OF

SHAKESPEARE'S SONNETS.

BY RICHARD SIMPSON.

LONDON:
N. TRÜBNER & CO., 60 PATERNOSTER ROW.
1868.

PREFACE.

The following chapters are reprinted from *The Chronicle*, where they first appeared. They were compiled from collections made long ago as notes to Shakespeare's Sonnets, and it is hoped that as they stand they will be of some use in pointing out the sequence of ideas in a poem which both needs and rewards the pains of a commentator.

Clapham, *February* 17, 1868.

CONTENTS.

CHAP.		PAGE
I.	THE SHAKESPEARIAN LOVE PHILOSOPHY	1
II.	THE ANALYSIS OF LOVE	16
III.	THE THREE PHASES OF LOVE	27
IV.	THE TRUE ORDER OF THE SONNETS	36
V.	IMAGINATIVE LOVE IN THE SONNETS	47
VI.	IDEAL LOVE IN THE SONNETS	60
VII.	VULGAR LOVE IN THE SONNETS	70
VIII.	CONCLUSION	75

THE PHILOSOPHY

OF

SHAKESPEARE'S SONNETS.

CHAPTER I.

THE SHAKESPEARIAN LOVE-PHILOSOPHY.

IN default of direct information, the student of Shakespeare's philosophy will naturally first turn to his lyrical poems. The epic poet relates facts as he finds them in story; the lyric poet reveals his own feelings, and the motives of his own thinking and acting; the dramatic poet is both epic and lyric—tells the story like the one, and, like the other exhibits his dramatic persons acting and speaking in obedience to the inner springs of their natures. Hence the lyric poet is most purely personal, because he is consciously and intentionally exhibiting himself. But the dramatic poet is personal too, because the thoughts and feelings which he puts into the mouths of his characters are all ultimately drawn from his own consciousness. Not that these characters can be taken as representations of what their creator is. Their production reveals, not what he is, but what he feels he might be, or should be, if he were not himself. If Shakespeare had been Othello, or Iago, or Hamlet, or Falstaff, or Henry V., or Hotspur, he might have acted and thought as they do in his dramas. But then he was himself, and not another. "I am that I am," as he says in one of his sonnets. Hence the knowledge of what he might have thought and done if he had been other than himself affords no obvious clue to the knowledge of what he, the actual Shakespeare, really thought and did in his own person. We will therefore dismiss his dramas, and examine his lyrical poems.

Among these the sonnets alone are purely personal. The *Venus and Adonis* and the *Lucrece* are dramatic stories, bringing out moods of feeling and thought with lyrical delicacy, but still moods which are completely external to the author. In these poems the poet goes out of himself; so he does in the *Lover's Complaint*. But in the sonnets it is the poet who speaks; it is himself whom he describes. And though some of the facts presupposed in certain sonnets may have been purely imaginary, still there also it is the man Shakespeare who professes to tell us his feelings and ideas in regard to relations which, though imaginary, are so natural, that personal character is almost as easily manifested by his determinations how to act on the supposition of their reality, as it could be by his action in real circumstances. For in these sonnets Shakespeare is not telling us what he should be if he were Iago or Othello, and not Shakespeare; but what he should be if, remaining what he was, he were placed in certain imaginary relations with others.

If this were all, we might approach Shakespeare's sonnets with some chance of finding there the feelings, dispositions, and judgments of the poet himself. But when we examine them we, first of all, find them so monotonous, so limited in their range of subject, that there seems little to be gained from them of insight into the myriad-minded man. And then comes in the thought that the sonnets are not strictly original, but mere echoes—that all the great poets who expressed themselves in this kind of verse used it as a recognized medium of a special kind of philosophy. This was so notorious that students of this philosophy had made sonnets the usual texts and subjects of dialectical discussion. In the nineteenth century it would be thought superannuated trifling to wrap up in, or to extract out of, what seems a mere love song anything deeper than its superficial sense. We may read Dante's or Petrarch's poetry as we listen to Handel's or

Beethoven's music, thoroughly enjoying the emotions it excites, but never seeking in it for the key to the mysteries of the world and of life. We should as soon think of extracting philosophy out of a nursery rhyme. But even this seeming absurdity is none. The nursery rhyme is a deposit, a fossilized remnant of an extinct philosophy. Philosophies pass through three grades. First comes the earnest, or religious grade; next the mythological, or poetic grade; last of all the old woman's, or children's tale. Grimm's nursery tales were once the legends of a theology; they next gave form to the imaginations of a whole people; and they have finally degenerated into what they are. Thales first reverenced water as the origin of all things; Pindar used the philosophy of Thales as poetical machinery; but now it could be turned to no practical purpose but to point a joke. In the same way the love-philosophy was in its full earnestness in Plato and Dante; it became poetry in Petrarch and Shakespeare; and it became an ironical subject for an amusing essay in Burton. As serious men extract primeval mythology out of nursery tales, so, if we wish to comprehend the philosophy of the old sonnet writers, we must put our minds into sympathy with their pretensions, and admit their claims to be the teachers of the men of their times, who did, in fact, make their works the text-books of studies as serious as that of Aristotle in the mediæval schools, or that of natural science in the present day.

The great poets claimed to be teachers of wisdom, and not merely exponents of feeling, and their contemporaries admitted the claim. Dante makes Virgil his ideal sage, and, in dedicating the opening cantos of his *Paradiso* to Can Grande, tells him that in his poem, as in every doctrinal work, the reader must diligently note six things— the subject, the agent, the form, the end or object, the title, and the kind of philosophy; after which the words themselves have to be interpreted in their three senses, literal, moral, and anagogical. His two philosophical works, the *Vita Nuova* and the *Convito*, are simply commentaries bringing out the recondite meaning of his own sonnets and canzoni. When certain physicians and natural philosophers disdained poetry as no real science, Petrarch defended it. "The business of the poet," he wrote, "is not to feign, in the sense of lying, as the unlearned suppose, but to feign (*fingere*) in the sense of putting together and beautifying; to adumbrate the truth of things moral or natural in artificial colours, to cover them with the veil of pleasant fiction, on the removal of which the truth shines out, with all the more interest in its discovery because of the difficulty of the search." (Opp. p. 905, Basil. 1581.) The poet "bodies forth" the spiritual essence of truth; and the philosophical critic in turn has to strip off the crust of sensuous external metaphor, and exhibit the poet's truth that lies beneath. Similarly Santillana, the Spaniard, defines poetry to be "an invention of useful things, which being enveloped in a beautiful veil, are arranged, exposed, and concealed according to a certain calculation, measurement, and weight." (Apud Morley, *History of English Poetry*, i. 31.) Montaigne even goes so far as to say that philosophy is little else than a kind of sophisticated poetry.

And the poets were accepted as masters of thought and science. Professors' chairs were founded in Italian universities for the sole purpose of expounding Dante; and there is a whole branch of Italian literature which consists solely of comments upon Dante, Petrarch, Casa, and other sonnetteers. In the sixteenth century literary society in Italy appears to have been broken up into small associations called academies, which met generally to listen to a new sonnet, or to a lecture on some old one. Many published commentaries on Petrarch appear to be notes of similar lectures. The most considerable names are found among these commentators. The only Italian treatise in the works of Pico della Mirandola is a system of philosophy in the form of a comment on a canzone of Benevieni. Some editions of Casa's poems contain a lecture by Torquato Tasso on the sonnet

> Questa vita mortal, che 'n una o' n due
> Brevi e notturne ore trapassa, oscura
> E fredda.

The two hours, says Tasso, mystically mean our irrational and our rational life. Some, he says, only live the life of sense, the first hour; others open their eyes to intellectual things, the second hour. For this he was taxed by a subsequent lecturer in the same academy with making Casa say that our intellectual life was cold and dark, one of our nocturnal hours. Such was the kind of disputation then fashionable. It is worth observing that Tasso divides intellectual men into two classes—those of original genius and those of artistic culture; the latter he divides into imitators and critical investigators. Thus he distributes the world of letters into three grades—the gods, the imitators, and the commentators; and we see that its common life consisted in meetings of academies to hear the poems of the imitators and the lectures of the commentators.

This fact explains one of Shakespeare's dramas. *Love's Labour's Lost* exhibits the Court of Navarre forming itself into "a little academe," the members of which wrote and recited sonnets, and commented upon them. Shakespeare's own sonnets were evidently written under similar circumstances. They are first mentioned by Meres in 1598, who calls them Shakespeare's "sugared sonnets among his private friends"—a circle, it may be presumed, like the Navarrese academy, or like the company of "enthralled souls" to whom Dante proposes his theorems in the sonnets of the *Vita Nuova*. When we think of this, we need feel no difficulty about the interpretation of the dedication which Thomas Thorpe the publisher prefixed to the first edition of Shakespeare's sonnets in 1609. "To the only begetter of these insuing sonnets, Mr. W. H., all happiness, and that eternity promised by our ever-living poet, wisheth the well-wishing adventurer in setting forth.—T. T." As the sonnets are addressed partly to a man, partly to a woman, Mr. W. H. (whoever he was) cannot have been their only begetter in the sense of sole parent, sole inspirer, or sole object; and the only alternative that has been thought of is to suppose that "begetter" means collector. But W. H. was something more than the collector; it was to him, Thorpe implies, that the poet had made the promises of eternity with which the sonnets abound. Even the later sonnets, then, if not written to him, were written, not only for him, but under his influence. So he was not merely one the dumb eloquence of whose beauty had forced Shakespeare to write to him; but one whose arguments and disputations provoked the poet to embody his conception of the "two loves, of comfort and despair," in his magnificent series of sonnets. We imagine W. H. to have been either the Earl of Southampton or some other young man of birth and wealth, wit and beauty, who had travelled into Italy, and had come back brimming over with academies and love-philosophy, with Petrarch and Platonism, upon which he disputed with Shakespeare, and by his discussions begot the sonnets.

Shakespeare is always a philosopher, but in his sonnets he is a philosopher of love. All the great sonnet writers affected one particular philosophy, which was derived originally from the *Banquet* of Plato. Socrates was supposed to be the first founder of this school of thought, and Shakespeare's adherence to it was so notorious that he was called in his epitaph "Socrates ingenio," a Socrates in his turn of mind. "I declare," says Socrates in the *Theages*, "that I know nothing whatever, except one small matter—what belongs to love. In that I surpass every one else, past as well as present." In the Platonic philosophy this "small matter" enlarged itself into the great sustaining force of the universe, and he who knew love knew the kernel of all that could be known. From the Platonic schools and books this science passed to Dante and Petrarch, and became a distinguishing characteristic of the Italian revival of the sixteenth century. From Italy it radiated through Europe, and was taken up by Surrey and Spenser. But it was treated by none with such depth and variety as by Shakespeare, who has devoted all his sonnets and poems, and perhaps half his plays, to the subject.

The Platonic philosophy, as adopted by the sonnet writers, discussed the matter and method of love. For its matter, love is the passion for the beautiful, or rather, as Plato says, for begetting or creating in the beautiful. Love is an act of the mind, excited and solicited by a beautiful object, and having for its object the production of a new beauty in, and by means of, the old, or already existing, beauty. Beauty, on the other hand, is that quality which renders anything an object of love. Truth is understood by being true but loved for being beautiful. Beauty is the only metaphysical quality which can become an object of the physical sense. Thus it is both physical and metaphysical; and love, the passion which it excites, appertains to both spheres—that of matter and that of spirit. It is this community of love which enables it to assume the character of universality. It is both material and spiritual, both active and contemplative. It comprehends the whole movement of the universe—its generation, upholding, and progress. It lies at the foundation, not only of every act of every agent, but also of the eternal creative act which brought into being, and still upholds, the whole variety and diversity of the two worlds of things and ideas. Love is a word which in this system equally describes the transcendental action of God, the intelligent activity of man, the sensitive activity of the animal, the nutritive activity of the plant, and the chemical or mechanical activity of inorganic elements and masses. Such is the doctrine of Boethius and Petrarch. Love is theology, logic, morals, politics, natural history, and astronomy. It is the sphere of which all sciences are superficial segments. Apprehension affirms all; Reason doubts or denies all; but Love reconciles all. It is a kind of prelude to Hegel's idea of the universal Becoming, of which Being and not Being are the two moments. It is the principle in which all contradictions find their ultimate solution and reconciliation; which restores sameness in differentiation; which maintains identity in spite of distinction, and fuses together subject and object, mind and matter, perception and thing, the ideal and the real. This conception of love imparts a special ethical character to the love philosophy. Its great mark is toleration. It does not fix its view on isolated truths, nor does it regard truth as consisting of a multitude of independent truths; but it looks at truth as a system which comprehends all realities, and in which every comprehended part is in mutual connection and dependence. For it, good and evil are not different substances, but evil is good misplaced. In things evil there is a soul of goodness; and reformation consists, not in annihilating the evil thing, but in translating it—in developing that soul of goodness within it which gives it life and vigour, and in directing it to the good which it erringly seeks. Hence, in all controversies it finds room for both the rival doctrines, instead of exaggerating one like the fanatic, or losing both by seeking the *via media* between them like the eclectic. For there is a point where contradictions cease to be mutually destructive, and coalesce like concave and convex, the inside and outside of a bowl. This ethical character of the love philosophy may be expected to remove the philosopher from any very conspicuous part on the world's stage. His theories are impracticable, however beautiful as dreams. Petrarch was a thorough specimen of the kind: "A scholar, or rather a woodman, a solitary wanderer, spouting my rough eclogues under the tall beeches, or, with greater presumption, tempering my fragile reed under the bitter laurel, more fervent in working than happy in my works, with more love of literature than knowledge of it. No sectarian, but hungry for truth, the difficulties of which, coupled to my weakness and ignorance, and my fear of entangling myself in errors, make me often embrace doubt itself for truth. Thus I, a unit of the multitude, the lowest of the low, have gradually become an Academician, attributing nothing to myself, affirming nothing and doubting of everything, except that which I consider it sacrilege to doubt about." (Petrarch, *Rerum Senilium* Lib. I. Ep. V. Opp. p. 745.) The former part of this description fits Shakespeare as he appeared to Jonson and Milton; the latter fits him as he is characterized by modern critics.

The history of human culture separates into two great divisions. In the first, the laws of the movement of the world are sought in causes of which man, through his creative activity, is conscious. In the second, they are sought in phenomena which are independent of him. In the first division, the encyclopædia consists chiefly of human sciences — logic, psychology, ethics, language. In the second, it consists chiefly of the inductive or natural sciences. The love philosophy belongs to the first æra. For that, as well as for the second, the great problem of philosophy is to find a universal principle or notion which unites and comprehends in itself the unity and diversity of the two worlds of matter and mind. But it could only be in the first æra that love should be supposed to be this principle. The love philosophy belongs to a period when the mind of man was supposed to have a real action on matter; when, by a concentration of will or the due enunciation of magic spells, material effects could be produced. In such a state of opinion love would naturally appear to be the principle that solves the contradictions of things, and shows how contraries can be united into a single and ideal whole. It was thus understood by the philosophers whom Phædrus quotes in Plato's *Banquet*; by Empedocles, who explained the evolution of all things by the play of three forces—necessity, love, and hatred; by Aristophanes, who sang "There were no gods till Love mingled all things; and by the mixture of the different with the different Heaven came to be, and Ocean, and Earth, and the undying race of all the blessed gods." Love was a principle which animated even lifeless things. All were urged on by a blind instinctive desire towards their natural end. Good was defined to be "that which all things tend towards" or "covet," and the chorus of schoolmen respond to Aristotle—"The appetite of each thing has its term in the good. All things, even those which are unconscious, desire the good." Love, the root and queen of appetite, was for such philosophers the law of the universe—as Boëthius says:—

> Hanc rerum seriem ligat
> Terras et pelagus regens
> Et cœlo imperitans amor.
> Hic si frena remiserit
> Quidquid nunc amat invicem
> Bellum continuo gerit;
> Et quæ nunc sociâ fide
> Pulchris motibus incitant
> Certant solvere machinam.
> (Boët. *de Consol. Phil.* ii. met. 8.)

And Petrarch (Opp. p. 614): "Great and wonderful is the power of love, which so mightily and so fast binds the least to the immense by an invisible but not insensible union, and rules with equable force things between which there is no parity. What a scope must this principle have in men who are rational and sensible, when it can bind together even the brute and incongruous elements of nature! The air would not unite with the fire, nor the earth with water; rivers would not know their banks, nor the sea its shores, nor the stars their courses, unless the almighty and sacred universal Love tied them together. . . . It is his privilege to make the unequal equal, and to cause the faithful lover to be loved in his turn." Thus love appeared to the philosophic poet to be the one principle in which all contradictions were solved—the great affirmative which swallowed up all negations, and, for its votaries, held the secret key which unlocks all the treasures of knowledge.

Such is the substance of love according to the Platonic sonnetteers. For its method, the Italian academicians give, after Plato, a ladder of six steps or degrees, by which love ascends from its imperfect beginnings to its complete end. The first step belongs to the outward eyes, the second to the inward eyes of memory. In the third step the memory merges into reason, and the imagination of visible beauty becomes the universal idea of material beauty. The fourth step begins a new series; the mind contemplating the idea of beauty contemplates itself, the ideal beauty is found to be in and of the mind, and thus the love is transferred from body to soul, from material to intellectual beauty. In the fifth step the intellectual vision, which, up to this point, is only conversant with the individual soul and its idea of beauty, receives "the light of beauty in itself," by becoming able to perceive the beauty of minds. The last step is when the loving soul gathers up all the degrees and differences of intellectual beauty in one all-comprehending divine mind. (Crescimbeni, *della Bellezza*, p. 14.) These six steps are grouped in two sets of three. First, love guided by the outward eyes devotes itself to the visible beauty which happens to strike it. Under the guidance of the memory this beauty becomes generalized; it is stripped of the accidents and particularities of perception, and love becomes fancy. Under the guidance of the idea, love becomes devoted to the one object in which it sees or imagines all the imaginary properties of beauty to be individualized. Thus, it begins with *any*, passes through *all*, and ends in *the one*. And now begins the second triad. The one in whom the whole idea of sensible beauty is individualized only represents such beauty to the mind of the lover; apart from him, or in relation to the eyes and minds of others, the beloved object is but one of many, undistinguished from the rest. Hence the idealized individual is contemplated, not as he is in himself, but as he is represented in the idealizing mind. This is the fourth step, wherein, by a kind of intellectual sense, we get to the love of the beauty here and now present in the mind that loves. Next, by a kind of intellectual memory, we get to generalize this individual mental beauty, and it becomes the beauty of all minds. Lastly, the general idea is once more individualized, and we love the beauty that is at once universal and singular—the Divine mind. Thus the three last steps correspond to the three first; and the intellectual love, like the sensible, begins with *one*, progresses through the *all*, and at last reaches the *all in one* and *one in all*. Thus, the scale of love corresponds to the scale of logic—simple apprehension, judgment, and reason—and gives a prelude to the movement of the Hegelian category—*Identity, Difference*, and *Community*. We have, first, the apprehension of beauty through the eyes, the judgment of beauty in the memory, the reason of beauty in the ideal; and, again, the apprehension of beauty in our own soul, the judgment of beauty in all souls, the reason of beauty in the one all-embracing soul. Such is the universal process of reason. First, the idea is conceived in its rough and primitive unity; next it is dissipated into fragments and parts; next these fragments are reunited into an organized whole. Like love, all thinking depends on these pulsations of the mind—these alternate expansions and contractions of the intellectual lungs.

This "ladder of love" deserves to be more closely contemplated. Its first stage is the birth of love through the eyes. A beautiful face arouses the attention like a cymbal's clang; the eyes anchor upon it; and love is born. This is a simple affair. The next question is, what is to become of love when the eyes are closed, or removed in space from the face they feed on? Love, if it is to last, must enter upon a new stage; from sight it must deepen into memory. Hence comes the necessity of absence for the true development of love. "Will you deny," says Petrarch, "that absence has its own pleasures? Unless perhaps you would confine the whole of love's wide empire to the eyes alone, and take it from the mind, which is its proper seat." Absence becomes the condition of the second stage of love. It leaves the memory free to act; and the memory looks through the eyes for all tokens that can remind it of the absent object. And anything serves the memory as a reminder and a comparison. Such comparisons are impossible without absence. Memory is at the same time forgetfulness: without forgetfulness memory would be undistinguishable from perception: it is the alloy of forgetfulness that robs its images of individuality and definiteness, and gives them that indistinctness which makes them into general representations which fit a whole kind. Forgetfulness also purifies the conception by lopping off the less striking accidents, and leaving nothing but the nucleus. The beautiful face fades away into an inconstant conception of beauty, which attaches itself to every beautiful image which the eyes present, and enables the mind to treat every such image as a symbol and token of the absent loved one. Thus the same poet who in presence of his mistress may have said, "Your eyes are not like stars, nor your neck ivory, nor your lips like roses, nor your breath that of violets," in her absence may, without inconsistency, ransack Nature for comparisons, and use up all the splendours of the universe to enhance or patch up the lapsing memory of her beauty. By this means a true analysis of beauty is forced upon the mind. Love, which in the first stage is intolerant and exclusive, and recognizes no beauty but that of the beloved face, is now forced to recognize beauty in all things, because memory sees the beauty of that face hinted at and reflected in so many forms. And now the lover undergoes his first trial, the trial of his constancy. The inconstant lover is seduced into worshipping all these new manifestations of beauty for themselves, forgetting that they should be to his heart only a mirror of his mistress. The constant lover does not refuse them his worship, but he gives them only a relative cultus:—

"You away,
As with your shadow I with these did play."

Constancy gathers up, in the idea of the chosen object of affection, all the scattered rays of beauty which it perceives in the world. Inconstancy allows the sight to overcome the memory, and the present beauty to blot out the absent one. Then to the constant lover absence demonstrates that he can see his beloved across "large lengths of miles;" that his mind and senses are no longer entirely his own, but have in a manner left him to reside with her; and that he has thus, in Platonic phrase, in part died to himself that he may live with her. Persuaded that his affection is returned, his life and his mistress's are no longer single.

Each lives in the other, and in that new home "thinks, and acts, and maintains his own being;" as Crescimbeni says:—" Thus he comes to live also in himself no longer alone, but in company with the soul of the beloved object, which passes into him as his has passed into her; so that, by his loving death, he has gained not one, but two lives." This ethical doctrine of the identification of the lover and the beloved is the counterpart of the logical doctrine of the identity of the knowing and the known. "The mind is the man," says Bacon, "and the knowledge is the mind. A man is but what he knoweth. The mind itself is but an accident to knowledge; for knowledge is a double of that which is; the truth of being and the truth of knowing is all one." As the mind takes a new form with every change of knowing, and the thing known takes a new form in the mind into which it enters; so the two loving souls have, as it were, suppressed themselves, and have enveloped themselves in a new existence, in which they live a double life in unity of being. This unity is the guarantee of constancy. All the scattered beauties which the senses collect are referred to the ideal beauty whose image lives in the memory, and are beautiful in proportion to their resemblance to it. And thus the three first steps of love in the contemplation of sensible beauty are completed.

The three higher grades of love begin with the conversion of sensible into intellectual beauty. Love is born in the eyes, but lives in the mind. It comes into being when it sees the beautiful face; but it lives on the beauty of the soul. Love does not decay with the decay of the sensible beauty which engendered it. It survives age and wrinkles. If it still lives when the beauty which begot it is dead, its life has clearly come to depend on some other beauty—on the beauty of the soul, no longer on that of the body. And this intellectual love goes through the same grades as the sensible love. It begins with the individual soul of the beloved one, as apprehended by the loving consciousness; it enlarges into love for the general nature of the soul, as distinguished by the judgment; and it perfects itself in love for the universal soul as comprehended by reason—for the universal soul, the "sacred universal **love**" which itself comprehends and **unites all** the differences of souls in general.

These two loves, the love of sensible and that of intellectual beauty, are **counterparts** of each other in their essence and their operation; their processes may be described in the same terms. If love begins with corporeal **beauty, it is, as Crescimbeni says,** not without the assumption that "beauty of body is naturally a conclusive argument of beauty of soul, because the one is only an offshoot of the perfection of the other, according to Ariosto's words:—

> 'Che se la faccia può del cor dar fede
> Tutto benigno, et tutto era discreto.'"

Such is the necessary **assumption of love in its lower grades.** Afterwards, when love is established, and is strong enough to go without supports, it **refutes the idea,** and even contrasts beauty of mind with **beauty of body,** confessing with Duncan that—

> there is no art
> To find the mind's construction in the face.

This **scale of love with its six steps may be** illustrated by the examples of **poets.** The lowest stage is the love of the concrete individual woman for her sensuous charm, **as in** the **poetry of Byron.** The second degree **is where** love is **eclectic, busying itself in a** subtle analysis of beauty, writing about blue eyes, or black hair, or **such component parts of** beauty in separate epigrams and **songs, as Herrick** does. In the third degree this analytical **process reunites** its scattered limbs, and the **lover worships universal** beauty either in the face, which is its **symbol, or in nature,** which displays it at large. Wordsworth's lyrical poems are in this grade. In the fourth degree, **or first step of** intellectual love, **the lover is** no longer taken **up with corporeal beauty, but with that of the mind and character;** the poet no longer remarks how the man looks, **but what** he is, and gives **us,** not a picture of his face, but of his personality. This **is** epic poetry. The next grade gives us a philosophical analysis of intellectual beauty. This is **the ideal of lyrical poetry.** The sixth grade puts together again all that was separated in the analysis, and contemplates that concrete intellectual beauty which comprehends every kind of beauty and perfection, that love which includes all other loves, that friend's soul which has become the symbol of the highest intellectual beauty, or that idealized action in which men combine to exhibit their individual characters. This is dramatic poetry.

This philosophy of love will be found to be a key to Shakespeare's Sonnets, explaining them as they stand, without obliging us to put them into a new and arbitrary order, or to invent biographical facts to fit their allusions.

CHAPTER II.

THE ANALYSIS OF LOVE.

LOVE, says Benedetto Varchi (*Lezioni d' Amor*, 2da parte, lez. 1ma, ed. 1561), being directed to the beauty either of the body or the mind, may be of the mind only, or of the body only, or of both. And this composite love, or love of both body and mind, may be of three kinds, according to the proportions of the composition. Love of the mind only, or intellectual love, is called the good dæmon or genius; love of the body only, or animal love, is the evil dæmon or genius. The three composite loves are not called dæmons, but only affections or passions. The first is noble or chivalrous love (sometimes called divine). It contemplates chiefly the beauty of the mind, regarding the beauty of the body only as a symbol of spiritual beauty, and employing only the two spiritual senses, sight and hearing. Civil, human, social, or domestic love, loves the mind best, but also loves the body, not only with the spiritual, but also with the material senses, but without overstepping the limits of modesty and civility. Vulgar or plebeian love is directed to both soul and body; but the love of body prevails, and it is loved for the sake of its own pleasures. As it is the function of love, Varchi continues, to beget beauty by means of beauty, the noble or chivalrous love, which loves mental beauty, and corporeal beauty only as its token, is more prone to devote itself to young men, whose minds, he says, are more apt to receive the beautiful impressions of virtue and science than those of women. The civil, and especially the vulgar love, on the contrary, being conversant more directly with corporeal beauty, are more prone to devote themselves to women than to men, who are, as Shakespeare says in Sonnet 20, nothing to their purpose.

It is the two dæmons of love, not the intermediate

passions, which Shakespeare describes in his sonnets. He says (Son. 144) :—

> "Two loves I have of comfort and despair,
> Which, like two spirits, do suggest me still;
> The better angel is a man right fair,
> The worser spirit a woman, coloured ill."

The intermediate passions—chivalrous love, domestic love, and vulgar love—are illustrated in his dramas and poems. The first series of sonnets is addressed entirely to the "man right fair," who represents the dæmon of intellectual love; the sonnets directed to him are passionate in their affection, but the affection is one of the purest friendship; and the twentieth sonnet, not without a certain coarseness of thought, entirely precludes any imputation of a Greek sentiment which would have at once changed the comfort of his love into despair. Shakespeare's conception will be made more clear by an extract from Pico della Mirandola's comment on Benevieni's Canzone. He notices that whereas Guido Cavalcanti made Love a woman, "Donna ti prega," Benevieni simply calls him Amore, as a man. The reason, he says, is that vulgar love holds the same relation to celestial love as an imperfect to a perfect thing; and the Pythagoreans symbolized imperfect nature by the female, and perfect nature by the male. Besides, he adds, vulgar love is more appropriately made conversant with females than males, because it is prone to material pleasures. Heavenly love, on the contrary, runs no such risk, but its whole bent is towards the spiritual beauty of the mind and intellect, which is much more perfect in men than in women. Wherefore the votaries of this love have, for the most part, loved some young man of generous mind, who enhanced the worth of his virtue by its union with corporeal beauty. They have not strayed after herds of loose women, who never raise men to any grade of spiritual perfection, but, like Circe, transform them into beasts. With such a chaste love, he says, Socrates affected not only Alcibiades, but all the most ingenuous and subtle young Athenians. So Parmenides loved Zeno, Orpheus Musæus, Theophrastus Nicomachus. Their intention was simply to make the corporeal beauty of those they loved the occasion of raising themselves to the contemplation of the beauty of soul, whence that of the body is an emanation and a consequence; and the beauty of the soul leads on to the beauty of angels, while from the angelic beauty we may rise to a more sublime degree of contemplation, and arrive at God, the first fountain of all beauty. This, he says, is the fruit which Plato sought from his love. Marsilius Ficinus notices that Plato, in the Phædrus, proposes three exemplars of love : one of woman to man—Alcestis and Admetus; one of man to woman—Orpheus and Eurydice; and the third of man to man—Achilles and Patroclus. In his mind, and, perhaps, in the general Greek notion, the last was the highest love; it was not feminine but masculine beauty that fired the imagination with the glowing sentiment and idealizing passion which was the stimulus of philosophy, and which raised a man above the vulgar and selfish pursuits of life, and even above the fear of death. With Plato, personal beauty was the one point of contact between the world of sense and the world of ideas. Justice and Temperance could clothe themselves in no visible shape, but Beauty became visible in the beautiful youth. With the vision of this corporeal beauty, love, he taught, begins; after a time it transfers itself to the mind and character of the beloved youth; by another step it passes over to the generalized idea of beauty in all objects, bodies as well as minds. Thence it enlarges itself to comprehend the worship of beauty in public institutions, in arts and sciences, till it ends in contemplation and worship of the self-beautiful.

That the love of man for man can be as ardent as that described in Shakespeare's sonnets, and yet entirely free from Greek corruption, is shown at length in Montaigne's Essay (Livre I. cap. xxvii.) *de l'Amitié*. His affection for Estienne de la Boëthie, which was a perfect community of soul and will, passing the love of women, is represented to be as ardent as that of Shakespeare for his friend. Sir Thomas Browne in his *Religio Medici* (Pt. ii. § 5, 6) hopes he does not "break the fifth commandment" if he loves his friend before the nearest of his blood. "I never yet," he says, "cast a true affection on a woman, but I have loved my friend as I do virtue, my soul, my God. . . . . . There are three most mystical unions—two natures in one person—three persons in one nature—one soul in two bodies. For though indeed they be really divided, yet are they so united as they seem but one, and make rather a duality than two distinct souls." And some of the earliest English poetry that is left to us consists of addresses to an absent friend, the tone of which reminds one of Shakespeare's sonnets. In the *Codex Exoniensis* (Ed. Thorpe, p. 288), is a poem called the Wanderer. In it the exile dreams of his absent lord. Then it seems to him

> "That he his lord
> Embraces and kisses,
> And on his knee lays
> Hands and head,
> As when he in former days
> His gifts enjoyed."

And in a similar poem (p. 442), "The Exile's Complaint," the solitary laments that although he and his lord had often promised that nought should part them but death, they have yet been separated, and nothing remains but sorrow, and the imagination of the absent:—

> "The far country!
> There my friend sits
> Under a rocky shelter,
> Whitened with storm."

With Plato, love is not merely the friendship which unites two persons by the bands of virtue and mutual kindness; it is also the passion for the infinite, the regretful reminiscence of something better than we see, and the presentiment of future immortality. Still in his estimation this high feeling is founded low down on the stimulus of passion. Love indeed, if it is to be perfect, suppresses this stimulus, or rather diverts it from its natural bias, and transforms it into something quite different. Yet Love is universally, in the highest and lowest forms alike, an impulse of generation. The impulse, in the brutal form, seeks only material pleasure; but as soon as it becomes human, it consciously seeks to bestow an immortality on what is mortal, to render lasting that which fades and dies. Its first human impulse is to produce a semblance of immortality by generating, through a person beloved for beauty, a new person, to replace the original one in its decay (Plato, *Sympos.* c. 32, p. 207), and thus to preserve the immortality of the species amidst the destruction of the individual. Of this impulse Beauty is the fuel; and love kindled by beauty is not precisely the love of beauty, but of generation in the beautiful. ἐστὶ γὰρ οὐ τοῦ καλοῦ ὁ ἔρως, ἀλλὰ τῆς γεννήσεως καὶ τοῦ τόκου ἐν τῷ καλῷ (*Sympos.* p. 206). It is the doctrine which Shakespeare puts into the two opening lines of his sonnets, to be as it were the text and motto of the whole—

"From fairest creatures we desire increase,
That thereby beauty's rose might never die."

The simplest and lowest form of this impulse manifests itself in the " vulgar love ; " it is purified and exalted in the " domestic " or " civil love ; " it is transformed in the " chivalrous love." For there the impulse is not towards the perpetuation of corporeal beauty, but towards the creation of mental beauty. The material sympathy is transfigured into intellectual union. Then comes the "celestial love," in those few privileged persons in whom the faculty climbs to the contemplation of beauty in its Idea ; when a man has attained to this, says Plato, he will have no eyes for the beauty of man or woman, or gold or colours (*Symp.* c. 35, p. 211). Thus of all love generation is the root and type. "When the fancy (says Messer Francesco Cattani da Diaceto, *I Tre Libri d'Amore*, L. iii. c. 3) conceives through the sight any vision which we pronounce to be beautiful, suddenly the mind desires not only to enjoy it, but to make it." This desire in the vulgar love and in the civil love is always material. But in the higher love, all that is material is suppressed, or rather transfigured and transformed into a purely spiritual act. Love has its roots in the earth, the corruption of which it has to suppress, and to transmute into the sweet flowers and fruit of art and science. An imperfect love fails to complete this transformation.

The "vulgar love" need not detain us. Shakespeare has thought it worth his while to devote a poem to it— his Venus and Adonis. The Lucrece is a contrast between the civil love of Lucrece and the evil dæmon of animal love which fires Tarquin. The later sonnets are also devoted to this animal love, which permits voluptuousness to overshadow and suppress the hope of increase. Their heroine is neither the wife nor the chivalrous mistress, but the tempter, the Cleopatra, the Cressida, the "bad angel" of the love of sense. But the contrast between the civil love and the chivalrous love is worth considering. The end of civil love is marriage; that of chivalrous love the connection between the *servente* and his mistress. The text book of this love is the *Codex Amoris*, attributed to King Arthur, but capable of showing no higher antiquity than Andrew, a chaplain of Pope Innocent IV. The Code contains thirty-one articles. The faculty for which it legislates is that ordinary love which has its roots in our sensual nature (Art. VI. Masculus non solet nisi in plenâ pubertate amare), and which might naturally and properly end in marriage (Art. XI. Non decet amare quarum pudor est nuptias affectare). Yet as the chivalrous love was quite distinct from civil love, it was therefore cut short in its development, and failed to attain its own special end if the lovers married. The only senses allowed to be the vehicles of chivalrous love were the eyes and ears. The lover was forbidden to go beyond gazing on, or hearing, or thinking of, his love. Two grades of successful lovers were acknowledged. A lover of the lower grade (the *écouté*) was initiated by the lady giving him gloves or girdle; one of the higher grade (the *ami*) by her giving him a kiss—the first and generally the last he could hope to receive from her. It is to this kiss that Art. XII. refers (Verus amans alterius nisi suæ coamantis *ex affectu* non cupit amplexus). On all other occasions chivalrous love was forbidden to transgress the strict limits of eyes and mind (Art. XXIV. Quilibet amantis actus in coamantis cogitatione finitur. Art. XXX. Verus amans assiduâ sine intermissione coamantis imagine detinetur). The chivalrous love of the woman was a kind of adaptation of the Platonic friendship between man and man to that between a man and woman, and a regulation of it by the forms of feudalism. The woman took the place of the feudal lord, the man that of follower. The office of receiving a knight as *servente* was a complete feudal infeodation; the vassal often called his dame *dominus*, and their relationship is said by M. Fauriel to have been sometimes blessed by the Church. When a knight was accepted as *ami*, he knelt before his lady, his two hands joined palm to palm between hers, and swore to serve her faithfully till death, and to protect her against all evil and outrage. She, on the other hand, accepted his services, promised him her tenderest affections, gave him a ring, and raised him up with a kiss. Chivalrous love was inconsistent with married love, because in marriage the chivalrous subordination of the lover to his mistress is impossible, the bounds of eyes and fancy are passed, and the life is domestic, not ideal. The lady is not supreme, nor her favours voluntary. The French knight in Fouqué's *Sintram* is not an accurate conception of chivalry. He would have had a mistress, but that mistress could not have been his own wife. His wife would have had her *servente*, but he could not have been her husband. There was no law of love more rigidly enforced than this by the Provençal Parliaments of love. Marriage between a *servente* and his lady destroyed the chivalrous relationship. On the other hand, no lady was allowed to give up a *servente* on the score that she was married to another. The first article of the Code defined that "causa conjugii ab amore non est excusatio recta."

The division between married and chivalrous love, which all the raptures and awe of fancy made necessary, was one quite in accordance with the habits of Southern Europe, but could find no real home among the Teutonic races of the North. In the Greek the love of women was either the natural impulse or a domestic relationship, never idealized or refined beyond the limits of the utilitarian, the commonplace, the unenthusiastic. She was either ἑταίρα for pleasure, or παλλακή for body servant and nurse, or γυνή for housewife. But the Germans had a kind of religious veneration for women, very far surpassing these utilitarian limits. This veneration they were able to preserve intact even in the marriage state. But to the Southern imagination such a combination seemed preposterous. It could receive from the Germans their woman worship, but could not allow it to be a wife worship. The Southern idea of marriage was, that in it the man sought a mother for his children, a housekeeper, a stewardess, but not necessarily a companion to share his joys and sorrows, or a friend to commune with his thoughts: still less a mistress in the chivalrous sense, a suzeraine in whose presence the servente-husband was to exhibit the awe and terror prescribed by the Code (Art. XV. Omnis consuevit amans in coamantis aspectu pallescere. Art. XVI. In repentina coamantis visione cor tremiscit amantis)—whom he was to regard as the depositary of a kind of celestial force and grace, communicable to him by assiduous contemplation and fidelity to thoughts of love. It is only in the Northern imagination of Fouqué that marriage could consist with so extreme a relation as this. Familiarity would mar it. The domestic subjection of the wife would annihilate it. Yet it was the continual tendency of our English poets to change the mistress of chivalry into a wife. Mr. Morley points out many proofs that such was Chaucer's endeavour. M. Taine on the other hand says that the Earl of Surrey was the first to do so. Spenser (in the Amoretti) was probably the first who exalted a wife into a mistress. Fouqué completed the ideal in his French knight.

Shakespeare never gives us this ideal. Chivalrous love of woman is not an element of his world. Even the worshippers in *Love's Labour's Lost* look forward to marriage as the end of their hopes, and receive their year's penance with discontent. This is a significant fact in his biography. He probably resembled Michel Angelo, a man whose life was a dualism, in whom the artist was sharply separated from the house-father and the citizen. Michel Angelo's long correspondence with his nephew turns entirely on domestic matters, without a hint about art or philosophy. It exhibits him as the maintainer and ruler of his family, quiet, steady, cautious, practical, unsentimental, concise. If we want the other side of his character, we must turn to his sonnets. Shakespeare's characteristic suppression of the chivalrous love, with its fantastical rites, points to the same kind of character. If we had his letters to his wife, they would probably be entirely occupied with domestic or municipal affairs. We should expect no philosophy, no æsthetics, little historical gossip. We might find a close calculation of the net proceeds of one of his plays, but certainly no indication of the idea on which it was constructed. Yet great men strive to have some confidant to whom they may impart their ideas. It is their bliss to find one capable of understanding them, one to whom they may speak interjectionally, without measuring their words or completing their thought. But where is the great man to find his equal? Greatness is solitary. He is generally forced to content himself with the mere mask of intelligence, with the deep blue eyes of a confiding woman or an enthusiastic friend. Imagination must take the place of judgment, and the sign must serve instead of the thing signified. But the domestic relations of man and wife soon destroy the illusions of imagination, and no one is more exposed to be miserable than the artist who should demand from his wife intelligent sympathy with his thoughts as well as with his moods as a condition of marital affection. Shakespeare seems to have avoided this rock; Milton ran his ship upon it. Shakespeare kept his active affections for his wife and children, his home and town, and sought elsewhere for the recipients of his artistic sentiments. He was a Nestor as well as a Socrates and Virgil, and knew how to keep his domestic affections unentangled with poetical dreams, true to the plain, uncoined, and homespun constancy of his own Henry V.

And when Shakespeare suppressed the chivalrous love of woman, he extracted some of its peculiarities, and with them modified his Platonic friendship. In the Platonic idea the beloved one is a beautiful youth whose mind the lover forms—begetting a beautiful mind in his beautiful body. The lover gives all, the beloved one receives. But in the chivalrous idea the tables are turned; the lady, the beloved one, is the generous one, the dispenser; the Knight waits upon her bounty; her eyes are to him the source of all love, all knowledge, all strength; they furnish not only the stimulus which rouses him, but the light that guides him, and the end which blesses him. All this may be read in Biron's speeches in *Love's Labour's Lost*. Similarly in the Sonnets the male friend who takes the place of the lady is not the Platonic beloved youth into whom the lover pours out all his wealth of mind to educate and adorn his soul; but he is the "master-mistress," the feudal lord and chivalric mistress in one, the incarnation of beauty from whose eyes the lover derives all his strength, all his knowledge, and all his love. On the other hand, the Italian Platonists of the Renaissance, while they acknowledged the authority of Dante and Petrarch, yet really followed Plato only, and suppressed the chivalrous ideal. They admitted only two ultimate kinds of love, vulgar and heavenly. In vulgar love they admitted a kind of superiority in the mistress, because they found in her the force which moved the lover; but in heavenly love the lover is the superior, because it is the beauty of his own mind which makes him desire to produce beauty of mind in the beloved youth. In this relation the lover keeps the mastery; he gives, and is therefore the greater; the beloved youth is formed by him after his ideal of beauty. The lover bestows the form, the youth is the wax which he forms. The lover remains the man, the youth becomes the recipient like a woman. In Shakespeare, on the contrary, the lover not only becomes the vassal, as in chivalrous love, but he also becomes a woman, he takes a wife's position, the position of one on whom all the sacrifices are imposed, whose duty and happiness are self-renunciation, self-abnegation, perpetual fidelity, and life-long sacrifice: in a word, the position of one who conquers by submission and purity.

In every perfect man there is a feminine element capable of this development. In the highest state of prayer the Christian man as well as the Christian woman professes himself to be the spouse of the Lord whom he worships. In exalted friendship there is something of the same feeling, and the first series of Shakespeare's sonnets shows how, in his artistic friendships, he had cultivated his feminine element, and had nursed the woman within him. It was thus that he must have attained to the unique power shown in his plays, the power of painting women as no one ever painted them before or since. It was his own theory that each human being, man or woman, possessed both natures, masculine and feminine—the will and the feelings. Hence such expressions as "to play the woman with the eyes,"—"all my mother came into mine eyes, and gave me up to tears,"—"nature her custom holds, let shame say what it will; when these are gone the woman will be out." The motherly element is "shrewishness," (*Twelfth Night*)—"rash humour," (*Julius Cæsar*) —the *hysterica passio* which swells up to madness (*Lear*) —every "motion that tends to vice in man," (*Cymbeline*.) The two elements, one derived from the father, the other from the mother, Shakespeare seems to regard as everywhere present, sometimes one predominating, sometimes another, but never really divorced. A great "sensation" brings out the woman. Cymbeline, finding all his children again, cries out, "O what am I?—A mother to the birth of three." An occasion which calls for an iron resolution brings out the man. Coriolanus is said to stand "as if a man were author of himself, and knew no other kin." And Cleopatra says, "My resolution's placed, and I have nothing of woman in me." In the intellect itself Shakespeare sought these male and female elements. He makes Richard II. say, "My brain I'll prove the female of my soul; my soul the father; and these two beget a generation of still breeding thoughts, and these same thoughts people this little world." Not only are soul and brain contrasted as male and female, but the thoughts which they generate are themselves "still breeding," self-propagating, by a like contrast,—" no thought contented," none self-sufficient, each modified by another, and by this perpetual intercourse perpetually generating new thoughts.

Such was Shakespeare's theory; and the practice he founded upon it may be gathered from the Sonnets, where he exhibits the formation of the tender, gentle heart by the sufferings and contradictions of a patient love.

CHAPTER III.

THE THREE PHASES OF LOVE.

LOVE, as conceived by the philosophical sonnet-writers, has a twofold movement—one altogether internal, which may be called its mania, phrenzy, or enthusiasm; the other reaching from within outwards—its ecstasy. The first is the soul's warfare, and the manifestation of its strength; in the second the soul finds its peace and rest. The unloving soul is in a state of dull stupefaction; it is settling on its own lees. Love is first a disturbance and a change, a transformation worked by a thorough dislocation, and consequent rearrangement, of the forces of the soul pent up within herself. As in the shaking of a kaleidoscope, so in the soul shaken by the earthquake of love, the component elements change places, and enter into new figures, new combinations. Love is a revolutionary or volcanic force like that which gives a new conformation to a country or a new organization to society. But as peace is the end of war, so rest in its end is the object of the disturbing force of love; and this rest is found in the ecstatic movement, which wrenches the soul from itself and sends it to seek its true life in union with the object of its love.

Love is an act both of the intelligence and of the affection. In both aspects it has its three states—its original embryonic state of immobility, its mania, and its ecstasy. Intellectually the soul begins with a dulness which may be made perpetual either by clownish idleness, or by the leaden contemplation of universal plodding which "prisons up the nimble spirits," and dedicates itself to "slow arts" which "entirely keep the brain," and show no "harvest of their heavy toil," "save base authority from others' books." Love is the spirit whose incubation infuses the first vivific motion into the inert soul. When it enters true life begins, and

> . . . with the motion of all elements
> Courses as swift as thought in every power,
> And gives to every power a double power,
> Above their functions and their offices.

It stirs up the first mania in the soul. This mania or phrenzy was divided by Plato into four kinds—the prophetic furor inspired by Apollo, the mystic orgiastic mania of Bacchus, the poetic enthusiasm inspired by the Muses, and the supreme and mightiest mania of love communicated by Aphrodite or Eros. From all of them Plato held the greatest blessings to arise. He appealed to the universal conviction that they were something more noble than sound sense, and were direct gifts of the gods. Shakespeare, in the famous speech of Theseus in the *Midsummer Night's Dream*, only recognizes three of these phrenzies—those of the lunatic, of the lover, and of the poet; and, unlike Plato, he regards them chiefly in their intellectual aspect. He looks at them all as disturbances of the imagination or fancy, which in all three cases attains an exaggerated development, overshadows all the other faculties, and makes the man seem to be of "imagination all compact." He states the one law by which in all three cases the phrenzied imagination acts. The seething brains apprehend some feeling, for which the shaping fancy immediately creates some supposititious cause, which the cool reason, when appealed to, refuses to acknowledge.

> Such tricks hath strong imagination
> That if it would but apprehend some joy,
> It comprehends some bringer of that joy.

In these phrenzied states, the apprehended joy or feeling always comprehends or suggests as its necessary concomitant, or rather as its bringer or cause, an imaginary substance or force which insinuates the feeling into the mind. Thus the melancholy apprehended or felt by the lunatic comprehends or includes in itself the imaginary perception of "more devils than vast hell can hold:" the tender feelings which the lover apprehends comprehend, in the vivid impression which they make, the imaginary perception of a beauty in his mistress' brow which little corresponds to the reality; and the undescribed and varied emotions of the poet comprehend in their fiery luminousness imaginary typifications and embodiments of them, airy nothings, to which only his pen gives their place and their name, and with which he peoples the vacant spaces of earth and heaven.

But these phrenzies or manias have hitherto not broken the bounds of personality. They have mightily stirred up the mind; they have caused it to dilate and contract, to press forward, to spread itself abroad, even to occupy all space, all spheres of thought. But they have not sent it out of itself; they have not broken down the walls and barriers between it and outward things, they have not confronted it with external realities, and compelled it to test its conceptions by any standard other than its own caprice. Knowledge, Shakespeare tells us, is "but an adjunct to our self." A man can no more see himself in himself than his eye can look into its own depths without the reflective aid of a mirror. Where the self is, there the knowledge is; and the same mirror which enables a man to see himself, enables him also to see and measure his knowledge. Shakespeare by this does not seem merely to indicate that strengthening of our knowledge and belief which immediately makes itself felt when we can communicate it to another, or convince another that we possess it. Nor does he mean merely that the conceptions of the imagination, when under the spur of the phrenzies, are monstrous, empty, unregulated, false, till confronted with realities, and brought into harmony with them. He means, also, that the accurate, philosophical knowledge, the object of which is the contemplation and consciousness of ourself and of our own mental acts and states, does not begin its existence in the form of direct self-contemplation, but of self-contemplation in the mirror of external phenomena—

> For speculation turns not to itself
> Till it hath travelled, and is married there
> Where it may see itself.

Man's soul, in Shakespeare's conception, is an eye which sees not itself—is a mirror, a glassy essence, a retina void of forms till it is confronted with such forms as it can reflect. Thus all speculation becomes, in his terminology, "reflection," "reverberation," "communication," or community of the knowing mind with the known object. The mind is in darkness and ignorance till it is provoked not only by the presence, but by the reaction of external things. All its imaginary causes, all the fancied bringers or upholders which it assigns as the operators of the feelings which it apprehends, are nothing till they can be shown to be reflections of realities, brought back again to be tested alongside of them, and thus married to them. Where such union proves impossible, the fancy dies. If without the soul external things are imperceptible, unintelligible, and simply blank, on the other hand without external things the soul is blind. It knows its own acts just so far as they are reflected and embodied in objects which the senses can apprehend. And it knows the meaning, the worth, and significance of these objects only so far as they are married to the intelligent powers of the soul, so far as they come within the categories of its self-consciousness, of that intelligence by which the soul finds within itself the measure and likeness of all external forces. For this reason Shakespeare identifies love and philosophy. Love, which is the ethical union of one soul with another, is at the same time the intellectual marriage of the senses, the imagination and the reason with nature. Without it the plodding thought lives "immured in the brain." When love comes, the senses gain a new inquisitiveness and new sharpness, the ethical character new strength, the intellect new subtlety, new harmony, new rhythm. Lopsided nature is rectified—"study his bias leaves"—and makes the beloved object its book and its academy.

The intellectual side of love lies in its action on the imagination; the moral side lies in its power over those passions, fear and desire, which chiefly influence the will. Plato seems to have sought the beginnings of its beneficial action solely in the awe which it inspired. For him fear was, in a sense, the beginning of wisdom. He describes how the man, struck with the love-inspiring dart of beauty, first shudders, and is overcome with terrors, then reverences the beautiful object as a god, then again is heated with the emanation of beauty which he has received, and which refreshes the wings of his soul, opens their pores, softens the skin, and causes the feathers to grow once more.

Then he tells us how the whole soul boils and throbs, sometimes relieved with an interval of joy, then again tormented with the strangeness of the affection, and made phrenzied, frantic, and sleepless—wandering about and longing once more to see the beautiful object which has been the cause and is destined to be the cure of all these pains. In presence of this beauty, he tells us, the vicious part of the soul is humbled and puts off its shamelessness, and swoons through fear. And from that time forth the lover's soul serves the beautiful object with simple reverence and awe. With Sappho and poets of her school this excitement only enhances the downward tendency of unbridled love with an intoxication which drowns the reason. With Plato and his followers the excitement is laid hold of to make it a means of purifying the soul. He enumerates the signs of awe and terror, the trembling, the sweating, and the shrinking, which are developed by the agency of love, and declares them to be the signs of the struggle of the inferior and material part of our nature, which through the agency of love is being subdued and brought into captivity by the superior and spiritual faculties. In conformity with this the *Codex Amoris* (Arts. XV. and XVI.) declares the trembling of the lover to be the constant and indispensable symptom of true chivalrous love. Hence Dante in his *Vita Nuova* tells us how he fainted and swooned at the mere sight of Beatrice. For her presence was to him the frost and blight of all passion and unworthy thoughts; she inspired a flame which kindled charity, forgiveness, and humility in his heart; and her salute wrought in him an intolerable bliss, which vivified his soul, but made his body like a corpse. These "fallings from us, vanishings," seemed to be the death throes of the diabolic natures which possessed or obsessed the flesh. The awe, the trembling, the impotence of speech, the involuntary sighs and blushes, the sunken eyes and feverish pulse, were an index of the mighty struggle going on within, which was destined to transform the soul. Love thus became a kind of sacrament, with its outward signs and inward grace; and men went through its discipline of groans and fasting and watching, just as they might go to confession and perform their penances. The story of Don Quixote's devotion is only a slight exaggeration and caricature of the reality. Shakespeare does not drive his heroes into the desert, to meditate there in nudity on the virtues of their Dulcineas; but in his comedies he sets down as notes of love the same kind of ascetic practices, fasting and groaning, tears and sighs, waning flesh, unkempt hair, unheeded clothes. A lover of this kind walked apart, chewing the cud of fancy, keeping out of his mistress's view, and yet fancying that all he did had secret influence over her, and advanced his claims on her heart. Thus, the awe and tremor which Platonism treated as the symptom of a great internal struggle, had grown, under the artificial system of the romancers, to be a kind of magical charm, an affectation, a state not produced by any internal struggle, but assumed in the place of that struggle. In the Sonnets we have none of this. The tremor and awe of the lover, when we have them at all, are real effects of love, not its counterfeits. He is put beside his part like an imperfect actor; the abundance of his strength weakens him; he faints when he writes of his love. But the devotion and self-renunciation which his love inspires is a riper fruit of it than these merely physiological effects of nervous emotion.

The ethical ecstasy of love was its final stage, in which the lover ceased to be himself and lived a double life—lived in the bosom of the person he loved. Such phrases as "My heart is in thy breast," "Thy breast encloseth my poor heart," and the like, which now seem to us frigid conceits, were in Shakespeare's days warm with the blood of a still living philosophy, though he knew well enough the hyperbole they expressed:

> Thee have I not lock'd up in any chest
> Save where thou art not,—though I feel thou art,—
> Within the gentle closure of my breast.

And he justified the expression by insinuating a distinction between his own living and acting self and that soul of his which in the ecstasy of love had taken up its abode in his friend's breast:

> As easy might I from myself depart
> As from my soul which in thy breast doth lie.
> That is my home of love.

The ecstasy of love brings the lover into direct relations with the person beloved, and thus imparts to love a new

THE THREE PHASES OF LOVE.

character. Love, while it is only in the fancy, is foolish and fantastical. It is nothing till it is in the will, and till it fixes itself on a real object. But the love, the loving person, the passion, and the emotion of love may remain one, and yet be directed in succession to various objects, as it climbs the *scala amoris*, or degrades itself from a higher to a lower kind of love, or is obliged to change by the mere wane and waste of time. But the doctrine of the old sonnet writers was not that of Mr. Tennyson. He sings:—

> God gives us love; something to love
> He lends us; but when love is grown
> To ripeness, that on which it throve
> Falls off, and love is left alone.

They, on the contrary, held that when one object fell off, it only revealed a better and higher object behind it, on which the widowed love at once fastened itself, not faithlessly forgetting the object it had just lost, but finding it again in a better and higher form in the new object. This was explained intellectually to be a process of successive abstraction by Ficinus, who tells us to abstract from body its matter and place, and we have mind; from the form of mind to abstract change in time, and keep only the multiple composition, and we have angel; from angel to abstract the multiple composition of forms, and we have simple form, pure Light, or God. On the other hand it was explained to be a process of accumulation by Blosius, who finds in God every beauty that exists apart in angels, or souls, or men, or animals, or plants, or suns, or stars. But in neither system is the widowed love left alone; she ever finds her widowhood to be the occasion for a step upwards on the ladder of love. Thus, as Plato tells us in the Lycis, the affection can be transferred by association from its primitive object to new ones, and yet the primitive object will still remain the real one; the other objects only operating on the mind by recalling to it, and carrying it back to, its primitive love. Thus, the affection for the new objects, he says, is only the affection for the old one under other denominations and disguises. But this is only an analogous case; it happens when the absent lover clings to every show which reminds him of the beloved one, and declares of them all—

> They were but sweet, but figures of delight
> Drawn after you, you pattern of all those.

D

Here love lends itself to many collateral objects without being false to its great object. It is a higher stage when all collateral, all inferior objects are summed up in the main object, and live a second life in him. Thus, in Shakespeare's one friend all former friendships revive—

> Thy bosom is endeared with all hearts
> Which I by lacking have supposed dead,
> And there reigns love, and all love's loving parts,
> And all those friends which I thought buried . . .
> Thou art the grave where buried love doth live . . .
> Their images I loved I view in thee.

For love is by nature and by necessity progressive. It must ever be loving higher objects, or loving the same objects in a higher manner. First, it is born in the eyes, and enthralled to the outward show. Then it grows independent of the eyes; for absence proves that love ranges where the eyes see not, and that the image of the absent supplies for his presence. Then the lover comes to see that the real object of love is not exactly the unknown reality, the secret of which the beloved object carries in his own breast—for eyes "draw but what they see, paint not the heart"—but the image which exists in the lover's imagination. This stage of love is appropriately called "fancy." It is the activity of the feeling for its own sake —love enamoured of itself, and not yet solidly grounded— a Proteus—a wandering ship ready to anchor in any bay. It is naturally inconstant, for it bears its ideal within; and, in the phrenzied glow of its imagination, it can fit this ideal first to one real person and then to another—to a Hermia, and then to a Helena, and back again to Hermia. Fancy, however, cures itself; each change is painful and shameful; pain and shame on the one hand, and the joy of return on the other, change fancy to fidelity. Fidelity no longer loves merely its own ideal—an ideal that fits indifferently to all realities; but it loves an ideal that is found to correspond to one and one only—to one who satisfies the ideal, in spite of the wane of the corporeal beauty which first aroused the passion. The fancy with its corporeal images fades away; and love is found to consist in the marriage of true minds, in a mutual render, in a mental correspondence, on which, in spite of death and time, constancy stamps the seal of immortality, and completeness impresses the semblance of infinitude. For it gathers up all lesser loves into the one sovereign love, which thus becomes all in all; and the love of the known brother emerges through death into the love of the unknown God.

There is then a unity which underlies all kinds of loves, and allows us to speak of the highest in terms of the lowest, and of the lowest in terms of the highest. A Persian school of mystics is said to transform by its interpretation the Bacchic couplets of Hafiz into the most devout hymns. For there is a spiritual drunkenness as well as a material one; and the logic of one is like the logic of the other. The unity which unites all kinds of love is far more close; and the religious interpretation of the Song of Solomon must be far easier than that of Hafiz's anacreontics. On the first reading of Shakespeare's Sonnets we seem to see only the passionate love for an earthly beauty. The next reading may reveal to us that this love is as much directed to the beauty of mind as to that of body. A third reading begins to dim the personal outlines: the object of Shakespeare's love begins to expand into something more general, more universal than the individual friend—something to which immortality and infinity themselves are not strangers. As this gradual growth in meaning is strictly in accord with the precepts of the philosophy which Shakespeare followed, it would be absurd to overlook it, or to neglect the natural explanation which it gives for such scandals as have been extracted out of Sonnets 40–42, or out of the profane application of the words of the Lord's Prayer to an earthly love in Sonnet 108. Religious allusions may abound in the love-poetry of a Platonist without the slightest profanity; for they only express the poet's sense of the identity of love in all its forms, and the community and interchangeableness of the terms applied to its various phases.

Thus, love of all kinds goes through three phases; first it is dormant, then phrenzied, then ecstatic. And its end is the rest and peace of the intellect by marriage with truth and reality, or of the soul by its marriage with the objective mind. Both intellectually and morally it expresses the progress of the soul from infinitesimal beginnings to an end all but infinite.

CHAPTER IV.

THE TRUE ORDER OF THE SONNETS.

THE first edition of Shakespeare's Sonnets, though it carries no positive evidence of being issued under the author's superintendence, yet on the other hand bears none of the marks of surreptitious and unauthorized publication which are so conspicuous in the original quarto edition of the several plays. The printing is exceptionally correct for the time, and the book is dedicated by the publisher to Mr. W. H., the "only begetter" of the Sonnets, who is apparently identified as the man for whom the poet made all the promises of immortality which they contain. For him they had been written or arranged in definite series, intended to illustrate the progress of a known philosophy. There is no reason to suppose that, in delivering them to the printer, he would have broken their continuity and confounded their order; and we ought therefore to suppose, till the contrary is demonstrated, that the order in which they stand is that which was intended by their author.

It is true that most of those who have written on the Sonnets have taken it for granted that their order is merely accidental, and have therefore taken the liberty of arranging them in new groups according to supposed internal similarities, or external relationships to persons and events. But none of those writers who have thus rearranged them seem to have given themselves the trouble to enquire whether it might not be possible to explain them as a series in their present order. They have first of all assumed some theory—that the Sonnets are historical, or that they are mere versifications of separate sentiments—and have thereupon proceeded to group them afresh, according to the persons or events they are supposed to touch, or according to the sentiment each may appear chiefly to enunciate.

And yet, if these poems are examined in the light of the common sonnet-philosophy — of that poetical Platonism which had inspired compositions of this kind ever since their rise—their sequence is quite natural, and they need no new grouping to make them into a single orderly poem. Indeed, examined in this light, they appear to be articulated and arranged with rare subtlety and care. The most superficial examination makes it appear that the 154 Sonnets are divided into two series. The first, consisting of 126, is addressed to a fair youth; the second, consisting of the remaining 28, is addressed to a black-haired, black-eyed, and dark-featured woman. It further appears that the love depicted in the first series is a force ever growing, triumphing over obstacles, and becoming ever purer and brighter; while the love sung in the second series is bad in its origin, interrupted but not destroyed by fits of remorse, and growing worse and worse with time. Such is the general construction of the book of Sonnets. And Shakespeare tells us that his intention was to exhibit two such loves. The opening quatrain of the 144th Sonnet is as follows :—

> Two loves I have, of comfort and despair,
> Which, like two spirits, do suggest me still:
> The better angel is a man right fair,
> The worser spirit a woman coloured ill.

The two loves answer to friendship and concupiscence, the *amor amicitiæ* and *amor concupiscentiæ* of the schools. The former love has its revolutions, but each time it returns to itself with renewed strength : it is the true infinite—the circular motion which is both perfect and endless. The other love is the false infinite—the eternal alternation of yes and no, without any true progress or any attempt at perfection. It is fickle, false, and fraudulent—perverse, self-contradictory, and full of change. In it the sense and conscience are at war. Sometimes one triumphs, sometimes the other : there is, however, no definite victory, but a perpetual approach to the final despair of the conscience, and the wearied indifference of sense. In the two series of Sonnets these two kinds of love are put through their trials. The higher love undergoes its probation of absence, suspicion, jealousy, and error, and proves "that better is by evil still made better." The lower love undergoes also its probation. It also triumphs over jealousy, triumphs over the disenchantments of experience, triumphs over the principles of morals (Son. 129), over the unsustained struggles of good resolution (Son. 146), and over the stings of conscience, which it finally perverts and blinds (Son. 151). Although these two kinds of progress are treated in a form which is perfectly abstract and impersonal, nothing prevents our supposing that many of the illustrations may be historical—that real persons and real events may be often used as the materials for the philosophic edifice. The only postulate which the theory of the Sonnets here advocated makes is that they are in the first intention philosophical, devoted to the exposition of the received sonnet philosophy, and only in the second intention biographical or historical, and therefore using real events in complete subordination to the philosophical ideas.

This theory both requires and discovers that in both series of sonnets the same cyclic character is found; that the progress in both is similar; that sonnet answers to sonnet; and that the similar sonnets occur in the equivalent phases of each series. This relationship may be traced throughout; and it distinctly proves that the order of the sonnets in the two series is right, or at least that both series are arranged on one principle, striking "each in each by mutual ordering," so that one becomes the counterpart of the other, just as in the dramas the subordinate plots are counterparts of the main plot, which they imitate either directly, or ironically, or by contradiction. It is not unnatural that Shakespeare should employ this method both in his sonnets and in his dramas. The importance of such a double structure for the interpretation of the poems is scarcely to be exaggerated. By means of it the author in a great measure explains himself. He gives us a number of points at which the two series are in contact, thereby marking the main divisions of each series, its salient and significant points of transition, and its parallelism with the other. This parallelism can be readily shown.

As the first series begins with the desire of love to see beauty immortalize itself in its offspring, so the second begins with the confession that beauty is profaned and disgraced, and its offspring bastard. One begins with hope, the other with accents of despair, for the future of beauty. For the *amor amicitiæ* looks forward to eternity, the *amor concupiscentiæ* looks only to present pleasure, and is reckless of the future. This contrast is found in the two musical sonnets, No. 8 of the first series and No. 128 of the second. While in the former the poet ransacks the deepest mysteries of the art to find reasons and prescriptions for increase, in the latter the "wiry concord" only confounds the ear, while the thoughts are occupied with something very different from the music, the fingers and lips of the performer. The "expense of spirit in a waste of shame" which the 129th Sonnet declares the *amor concupiscentiæ* to be, is parallel with the waste of beauty, the ruin, the cold decay, the wastes of Time, the unthriftiness which in Sonnets 9—14 the poet charges on Beauty which is unwilling to fulfil the duty of self-preservation. In his eyes, if lust is "murderous," so also is selfish Beauty which does not care for posterity;—

> For thou art so possessed of murderous hate
> That 'gainst thyself thou stick'st not to conspire. (Son. 10.)

The next point where the two series approach each other is in Sonnets 21 and 130. The two are perfect counterparts; both turn on the same thought of the folly of racking invention to find comparisons for the object of love, and of turning heaven itself into mere paint to colour it. A person may be worthy of the highest love, or may deeply stir the lowest passion, and yet be nothing like sun, moon, or stars. The two following sonnets of the second series give this thought a development which it lacks in the first. Attractiveness consists in something different from resemblance to the great works of nature; even in something that is distinct from the usual ideal of beauty.

The next point of contact is in Sonnets 40–42 of the first series, and 133, 134 of the second. These so evidently refer to the same real or imaginary incident, that in all rearrangements of the sonnets they are put together. The earlier set is, however, clearly addressed to the "better angel," the later to the "worser spirit." The *amor amicitiæ* dies if it is not reciprocal. But the baser love asks for no such return. At least it demands no exclusive fidelity, but only so much compassion as will afford consolation to the lover's passion. Hence, the laxity of Sonnets 133, 134, which, however superficially resembling the earlier set (40–42), differ in this, that while friendship needs not be jealous of the friend who seeks not another friend, but only a mistress, the vulgar love may still have reason to quarrel with the mistress who is not only unfaithful to her lover, but also robs him of his friend. In the first series, though the lover is contented with nothing but his friend's whole heart, yet with this engrossing affection he not only earnestly invites him to marry, but expressly leaves him free in his relations to women.

Mine be thy love, and thy love's use their treasure. (Sonnet 20.)

The friendly love, as Shakespeare conceived it, has this in common with the chivalrous love—that it lives in a higher plane, which lies parallel with, without touching the inferior level of the civil and domestic love of a wife, or the vulgar love of a mistress.

The next place where the two series touch is Sonnet 57 with Sonnets 135 and 136. The two latter are superficially distinguished by the puns upon the name of "Will." In the original edition the final couplet of 57 is distinguished by the same character. Love is such a true fool in the heart of your *Will*, that whatever you do, he thinks no ill of it. In both places the lover expresses absolute humility, which dares not rise to jealousy. "Nor dare I question with my jealous thought where you may be," he says to his friend. Let none of your desires, no wish, be violently suppressed, he says to his mistress. Think them all one, merge them all in the unity of your will; and then let me, who am also a *Will*, approach you as an integral part of the whole. This communism of vulgar love is found equally in Donne, Elegy III. : "Women are made for men, not him, nor me." Constancy is no ingredient in this "love of despair." Its only eternity is an everlasting change, not an everlasting growth. As Donne says again, "Change is the nursery of music, joy, life, and eternity."

Proceeding onwards, the 137th Sonnet, though materially corresponding with two sets of sonnets in the first series— 43–47, and 113, 114, all of which refer to the violence which love puts upon the eyes so as to make them false, yet formally has much more real relationship with Sonnet 62. The "sin of self-love" blinds the eye in one case, and the sin of vulgar love blinds both eyes and heart in the other. The 138th Sonnet deals with false seeming and pretence in vulgar love in a contrary way to that in which Sonnets 67–70 deal with false seeming and false surmise in the love of friendship. The 139th and 140th Sonnets are the indubitable counterparts of Sonnets 88–90. In the earlier numbers the lover justifies his friend for wronging him, and invites him, if he intends to be faithless, to be so at once, and to put him out of his misery. He promises, however, to justify his friend's conduct, whatever it may be. In the later numbers the lover warns his mistress not to call upon him to justify the wrongs her unkindness lays upon him; he will do nothing of the sort, but will go mad, and slander her, if she does not at least pretend to be faithful to him. Sonnets 141–143 develope the two ideas of the falsehood of the senses and the madness of the judgment. The lover's fondness is a voluntary madness, of which he can give no account but this—"My heart is pleased to dote," and it makes him pursue his mistress as she pursues others, asking only to be accepted as others are, and to experience her kindness only in the intervals which she can spare from them. In the same spirit the lover, in the former series of Sonnets 92–94, wishes to be spared the knowledge of his friend's falsity, if he is false, wishes to live deceived, to enjoy a kind face if he cannot have all the heart, but at the same time warns his friend that his beauty is like Eve's apple, his lilies worse than weeds, if his virtue is not what it seems to be. Sonnet 144 has already been quoted as the key to both series. Its burden, in the latter part, is this— If the absent friend is playing false with the lover's mistress, she will "fire him out." The counterpart to this, in the first series, is found in Sonnets 109, 110, where the lover declares that his absence does not argue falsehood—

> . . . If I have ranged,
> Like him that travels I return again. . . .
> Those blenches gave my heart another youth,
> And worse essays proved thee my best of love. . . .
> Mine appetite I never more will grind
> On newer proof, to try an older friend.

His erring love, we see, has "fired him out," and made him return to his true love. After a brief and lyrical reconciliation with his mistress in Sonnet 145, and a new quarrel with himself, with a half promise of amendment, in Sonnet 146, the votary of the *amor concupiscentiæ* in Sonnets 147 and 148 recognizes afresh the feverish delirium and false seeing of his passion, in terms which are the very counterparts of Sonnets 113, 114, where the analogous false vision of the better love is discussed, and Sonnets 118 and 119, where the "sickness" and "madding fever" of passion, which have been a temporary barrier between the lover and his friend, are bewailed and excused. Then while in Sonnet 149 the baser love balances the unkindness of the mistress with the corresponding unkindness and self-torment of the lover, in Sonnet 120 the nobler love balances the unkindness of the friend with that of the lover, and proves the depth of the love by the torments mutually inflicted and endured. The lover tells his friend that his infidelity, rightly interpreted, is a proof of his love, and tells his mistress that the very falsehood of his senses should recommend him to her. It is necessary to bring together the two parallel Sonnets, 121 of the first series and 150 of the second, in order to understand the former, and bring it within the moral code of the higher love.

> 'Tis better to be vile than vile esteemed
> When not to be receives reproach of being.

In Sonnet 150 the lover complains that it is his mistress's very vileness and insufficiency that has enthralled him. So the lines quoted will mean, it is better in love to be really vile, for vileness itself will sometimes command affection, than to be esteemed vile and thereby lose all love. Lastly, a comparison between the concluding Sonnets of each series, 124, 125, and 151, 152 (for 126 is merely a tag or appendix to the first series, as 153 and 154 are to the second), will show how the higher love in its last development becomes sublimated into a religion, while the lower love perverts conscience and truth, the corner-stones of religion. In this unsatisfactory manner the poem of the love of despair closes. It has a bad end. Shakespeare was too good a philosopher to exhibit all paths as leading alike to bliss; but he shows how of the two kinds of love which he sings, one toils steadily upwards in spite of occasional lapses, the other rapidly descends in spite of occasional halts. One ends in independence of all the powers of change, that is, in immortality; the other in a slough of despair, in the self-condemnation of one whose intellect knows that his choice is evil, but whose will is too weak to revise it.

Thus a comparison of the two series of sonnets shows that they run parallel to each other; the first comprises all that the second possesses, and much more besides; for the love of friendship is treated more fully than the love of desire. To the first 125 sonnets are dedicated, to the second only 26. But these 26 are found to correspond with a proportionate number in the first series; and, so far as the parallelism extends, precisely the same order is found in both series. This is surely a great argument to prove that the sonnets remain in the order in which their author intended them to be read.

It will perhaps be worth while to exhibit in a tabular form the points of contact. The numbers in the first column refer to the sonnets of the first series, those in the second column to the corresponding sonnets of the second series. By a glance at this comparative table it will be seen that the two series are correlative, and both arranged on the same principle.

1-7	=127.	57	=135, 136.	113, 114 }	=147, 148.
8	=128.	62	=137.	118, 119 }	
9-14	=129.	67-70	=138.	120	=149.
21	=130.	88-90	=139, 140.	121	=150.
34, 35 } 40-42 }	=133, 134.	92-94	=141-143.	124, 125	=151, 152.
		110	=144.		

But again, if we examine the first series by the light of the Platonic "scale of love," we shall find that in its main outlines it rigidly adheres to the prescribed form. That scale, it will be remembered, treats of the transformation of love from a sensible impression to an ideal force. It has two great divisions: the first is imaginative love, the second is ideal love. Each of these divisions separates into three subdivisions. In the first division love is (1) born in the eyes, (2) nursed in the fancy through absence, and (3) generalized in thought. Then after the transition to ideal love, sentiment concurs with sense, the heart supersedes the eyes. In this second division (1) the heart, more truly than the eye, furnishes the idea; (2) the idea is purified in the furnace of jealousy; and (3) at last it is rendered universal and absolute in the reason.

These six steps are clearly marked in the first series of Shakespeare's Sonnets. First we have the love of beauty kindled through the eyes, and leading to the perfectly chaste desire of creation in the beautiful in Sonnets 1—25. The second step, that whereby the fancy or imagination becomes substituted for the eyes through the absence of the lover from his friend, begins with a solemn dedication in Sonnet 26, and continues to Sonnet 37. The third step, the triumph of fancy over absence, is introduced with another dedicatory Sonnet, 38, and continues down to 43. The two next Sonnets mark the transition of sense into sentiment, through the insufficiency of the sensible powers of imagination. With Sonnet 46 the second great division begins; the heart now shares its creative power with the eye, and the newly born ideal love feeds not so much on the imagination of beauty as on the conviction of the friend's worth and constancy. This first subdivision continues to the end of Sonnet 65. The next Sonnet begins the next stage; it is a general prelude to all the trials of ideal love. The ideal love is led through the chief dangers which beset it, which might destroy it if it yielded, while from their conquest it may acquire its triumph and its glory. Love has to struggle in succession with affectation, slander, death, jealousy, humiliation, and the feeling of utter unworthiness. This continues to the end of Sonnet 96. From thence to Sonnet 125 we have the triumph of ideal love, gradually transformed into a sentiment and volition undistinguishable from religion. For love is the faculty for the infinite, and whatever objects it seizes are invested, by the fervour of its imagination, with the attributes of the infinite. As the judgment gradually becomes clearer and cooler, each object begins to take its proper place, until love, perfectly purified, attaches itself supremely to that which is really infinite. The following table resumes the main divisions of the first series of sonnets according to the Platonic scale of love:—

I. 1. Sonnets 1—25.	II. 1. Sonnets 46—65.
I. 2. „ 26—37.	II. 2. „ 66—96.
I. 3. „ 38—45.	II. 3. „ 97—125.

It is natural that the second series of sonnets should not respond to the scale so clearly as the first. For the vulgar love is sensual, not ideal, and it is hard to see how it can be idealized. Yet we shall find that Shakespeare solves the problem. The first step, love through the eyes, is set forth in Sonnets 127–130. The second step, the transfer of love from the sight to the fancy, is included in Sonnets 131, 132. In the former the lover thinks on his mistress's face, in the latter he turns her black eyes into mourners pitying his condition. The third step, the generalization of fancy, is found in Sonnets 133, 134. The poet exhibits this stage of love by making his lover willing to share his mistress with his friend. The transition from the imaginative to the ideal is represented in even a stranger manner in Sonnets 135–137. "Will," the name of the lover, becomes identified with his mistress's will or volition, and his heart, in spite of his knowledge, is obliged to pass a false judgment upon her. The triumph of this false judgment over falsehood, inconstancy, slander, the disillusion of the senses, the consciousness of wrong, and every cause of jealousy, is shown in Sonnets 138–143. Finally the rest of the series, 144–152, exhibits the vulgar love in all its deformity as a "bad angel" (144), by turns coaxing and leading to despair, and gradually working up to a climax, till it becomes love in hate, with darkened and perverted conscience. The main divisions of this series of sonnets may therefore be thus exhibited:—

I. 1. Sonnets 127—130. II. 1. Sonnets 135—137.
I. 2.   „   131, 132. II. 2.   „   138—143.
I. 3.   „   133, 134. II. 3.   „   144—152.

Viewed therefore side by side, either in the light of their obvious parallelisms or in that of the Platonic *scala amoris*, the two series of sonnets, that which celebrates the higher love and that which celebrates the lower love, are perfectly symmetrical, and arranged in agreement with each other and with the scale. This fact proves beyond all reasonable doubt that the present arrangement is the right one, and by implication proves also the inadmissibility of any theory concerning them which postulates any change in that arrangement. The main outlines of the sonnets are clear. There may remain innumerable difficulties in detail, arising from repetitions, apparent misplacement of sentiments, anticipations in the earlier sonnets of ideas which ought only to be found higher up in the scale, and in the later sonnets reappearances of ideas which had been dismissed in earlier stages. But these difficulties arise from the nature of the subject. Love is continually bearing "the second burden of a former child;" and "as the sun is daily new and old," so is it continually "telling what is told." It is in continual revolution, the same side of the wheel turning up ever and anon, but each time with some new growth, some development, something better than at first. It is an undulation, in which each successive vibration grows stronger, but each resembles the other, and causes an appearance of monotony unless the gradual growth is well observed.

CHAPTER V.

IMAGINATIVE LOVE IN THE SONNETS.

WHEN Shakespeare had formed the design of exhibiting the gradual ascent of Love through each degree of its scale, from the first conception of fancy in the eyes to the final possession of the whole heart and intellect by ideal love, he naturally began with a definition of the force whose progress he was about to describe. Every word in this definition is accurate:—

> From fairest creatures we desire increase,
> That thereby beauty's rose might never die.

"Fairest," he says, because the lover attaches himself not to the fair in the abstract, but to the one fair which approves itself to him as the highest: "creatures," because love, defined as the "desire of generation in the beautiful," applies only to creatures subject to change and death. But this desire of generation is founded on another desire still more general; its roots lie in a still deeper ground, the desire "that beauty's rose might never die." The word "rose" here is full of import. In the range of its associations it reaches from the meaning that must be given to it in much of the *Romaunt of the Rose* to the sublime conception of Dante in the 30th and 31st cantos of his *Paradiso*. The aspiration for the immortality of the "rose of beauty" is the root of love. The aspiration, when kindled by the beauty of fading creatures, produces the desire of increase from the fairest of them. And the desire, when the lovers are man and woman, is the root of domestic love; and when they are both men, causes the lover to wish to produce an excellent mind in the beautiful body of the beloved youth. But this Platonic creation hardly satisfies the aspiration for immortality, for the mind disappears when the youth dies. Hence before Shakespeare's days there had arisen a current commonplace of friendship, by which one friend would urge another to marry and to transmit his likeness to posterity. Mr. Gerald Massey has pointed out that the advice of Cecropia to her niece Philoclea, in Sidney's novel of *Arcadia* (Book III. pp. 431, 432), contains not only the general sentiments of Shakespeare's first batch of Sonnets, but several of the arguments on which they are based. "As Nature made you child of a mother, so do your best to be mother of a child," is, *mutatis mutandis*, the last line of Sonnet 13. "You had a father; let your son say so." Sidney's simile of rose-water in a crystal glass is adopted by Shakespeare in Sonnet 5; his remark about the monotony of one string seems to have suggested Sonnet 8. But Sidney, like Shakespeare, was in this only an echo of his time. His friend Languetus had pressed him with much the same arguments which he put into Cecropia's mouth (*Langueti Epist.*, p. 197):—"If you marry a wife, and beget children like yourself, you will be a better servant of your country than if you cut the throats of a thousand Spaniards or Frenchmen."

In accordance, then, with the feeling of his age, Shakespeare makes this the first aspiration of the friend who has just been struck with the beauty of the youth he is destined to love. One of the Egyptian gods was armed with a whip with which he excited the Moon to scatter the seeds of fertility upon the earth. Of like kind is the first step in Shakespeare's friendship. In the first nine Sonnets he urges his friend to marry on general grounds; his neglect is wasteful, shameful, unjust, a malversation of trust, and a wilful dilapidation of an estate in which he has only a life-interest. Then with the 5th Sonnet begins a series of rhetorical arguments for marriage. First comes Sidney's crystal; then the same thought, coupled with others which we find in Marlowe's *Hero and Leander*, and which Parolles reproduces in Shakespeare's own drama of *All's Well that Ends Well*. The 7th Sonnet is founded on the converse of a proverb which was often in Queen Elizabeth's mouth when she refused to name her successor— "Men use to worship the rising sun." On the other hand, says Shakespeare, men turn their backs on the setting sun, and the only way to retain their homage is to receive it in the person of a son and successor. The 8th Sonnet is founded on an acoustic phenomenon which has excited so much attention that we may trace to it the invention of the harmonic stops on the organ—the twelfth and sesquialtra. If two strings sound any two notes of the perfect triad in complete accord, the third note will be spontaneously produced in the air by a complementary vibration. From this Shakespeare by an ingenious conceit draws an argument for marriage.

> Mark how one string, sweet husband to another,
> Strikes each in each by mutual ordering,
> Resembling sire and child and happy mother,
> Who all in one, one pleasing note do sing;
> Whose speechless song, being many, seeming one
> Sings this to thee: "thou single wilt prove none."

From this point the arguments become less rhetorical, and appeal more directly to the feelings. Do you keep single for fear of wetting a widow's eye? But the whole world will be a widow and weep if you leave no copy of yourself. You cannot love others when you commit this murder on yourself. In Sonnet 10, the poet first ventures to introduce his own personality; if you will not marry on other grounds, at least "make thee another self for love of me." In the 13th Sonnet he advances still farther. Now he calls his friend "Dear my love," and affectionately entreats him to reproduce himself; and in the 14th he declares himself prophet enough to know that truth and beauty shall thrive together if he will do so, but that if he will not, his end "is truth's and beauty's doom and date." Then come five Sonnets in which the poet, seeming to despair of being able to influence his friend's conduct, declares that he himself, by his verses, will confer immortality upon him. He will war with Time—"as he takes from you I will graft you new." You might make war on Time, he says, "a mightier way" and by "means more blessed than my barren rhyme," by begetting living pictures, "drawn by your own sweet skill." Without such witness of its truth, he says, my description of you will not be believed; with such witness "you should live twice, in it and in my rhyme." But, finally, casting away all hope of persuading him, he triumphantly announces his own power of immortalizing him—

> So long as men can breathe, or eyes can see,
> So long lives this, and this gives life to thee— ...
> —Do thy worst, old Time: despite thy wrong
> My love shall in my verse ever live young.

This was a common-place of sonnet writers. The fading beauty of the beloved was to have everlasting life in the poet's verse. Mr. Knight prints, in his illustrations of the Sonnets, similar sonnets of Spenser, Daniel, and Drayton, with remarks which show his unacquaintance with the philosophy common to them and most of the other great sonnet writers. They considered that Love, as Aristotle says, consists rather in loving than in being loved—that it is action rather than passive receptivity—that it gives rather than receives. The lover gives himself, and does so in order to confer immortality on the beloved. The soul, taken with the beauty of its friend, is seized with melancholy when it reflects that this beauty is only lent, not given, to the world; and its first aspiration is that such grace may never die. At first, while friendship is more in the wish than in the will, the incipient lover, with a kind of distant respect, only urges his friend to immortalize himself; failing in this, he proceeds, timidly at first, to associate himself with his friend, to express a more direct and personal interest in his existence, and to undertake something that shall immortalize him.

The highest expression of this friendship is doubtless self-sacrifice. "In quid amicum paro?" says Seneca. "Ut habeam pro quo mori possim, ut habeam quem in exilium sequar, cujus me morti opponam et impendam." In the first sonnet of the *Vita Nuova*, Love appears to Dante, carrying Beatrice sleeping in his arms, and holding the poet's heart in his hand. He wakes her, and feeds her with the burning heart, and then departs in tears. The poet asks his friends to interpret the fearful vision. Guido Cavalcanti alone solves it:—

> Your heart he bore away, for he perceived
> That to your lady Death was laying claim,
> And fearing this, sustained her with your heart.

To die for one's friend is the highest expression of friendship; but it does not satisfy the aspiration of love. A brief remainder of life cannot purchase more than it spends. The problem of love, as it proposed itself to the sonnet writers, was to find some surer means of giving immortality. Cicero says that of two friends, both live while one survives: for the dead still lives while his memory is preserved with veneration and tender regret in the bosom of the survivor. Sometimes the survivor can rescue his friend from evil report; and then it becomes his duty to live. Thus Hamlet says to Horatio, who was about to drink the remains of the poison—

> O God, Horatio, what a wounded name,
> Things standing thus unknown, shall live behind **me**!
> If thou didst ever hold me in thy heart,
> Absent thee from felicity awhile,
> And in this harsh world draw thy breath in pain
> To tell my story.

It was this immortality of Mnemosyne that the poet-lover appropriately sought to confer. The poet commemorates his friend, not in a way that costs nothing beyond a single resolution and a blow, but in words distilled with tedious labour from the very marrow of the brain and heart, in verses whose beauty captivates men, and which become a monument more durable than brass. Dante begins the *Vita Nuova* by offering his heart to preserve Beatrice; and he ends it with the resolve "to say that of her which was never said of any woman"—a resolve which gave birth to the *Divina Commedia*, in which her memory was embalmed and made eternal. In like manner Petrarch, who begins by protesting how incapable his lines are of expressing Laura's beauty, gradually finds that they confer fame upon her (Son. 39), and carry her name wheresoever the language is understood (Son. 96), and, after her death, boasts that they shall give her an eternal fame—

> E, se mie rime alcuna cosa ponno,
> Consacrata fra i nobili intelletti
> Fia del tuo nome qui memoria eterna. (Son. 55, sulla Morte.)

And in one of his miscellaneous Sonnets he tells Malatesta that poetry gives immortality in a way that no monumental bust can rival. Mr. Knight might have greatly enlarged his list of English poets who make the same boast.

The 20th Sonnet reverts once more, and for the last time, to the idea of corporeal reproduction. The poems which were to immortalize the beloved youth were in some sense his offspring, for they were inspired by his eyes— "from thine eyes my knowledge I derive." But yet the poet, in spite of the confidence which he expresses, feels diffident of his powers, and says, in effect—" You are so like a woman, that it is a pity you are not one. Nature, making you a man, deprived me of you. You should be my mistress; as that cannot be, your love may be mine, whether you devote yourself to women or not." This sonnet is a transition. Its familiarity marks a great advance in friendly intercourse, while the light way in which the friend's relation to women is treated in it marks both the abandonment of the persuasions to marriage, and the deficiency of moral depth in this early stage of friendship, which is at present a mere "fancy," bred in the eyes, and dependent on corporeal beauty, and the desire of immortalizing it. Behind the materialism of this love we see here and there a new element arising, the "gentle heart" unacquainted with "shifting change;" but this new element has not yet acquired any moral force.

From this time the love of the two friends becomes a reciprocal passion. In the 21st Sonnet the poet, having the reality of his friend's beauty before his eyes, refuses to compare it with sun, or moon, or gems, or flowers, but simply says that it is as fair as that of any mother's child, though not so bright as the stars. Shakespeare's own practice in Sonnet 98 seems contrary to the theory of this Sonnet, and of the similar one, 130, in the second series, till we remember the different positions occupied in the scale of love by this Sonnet and by No. 98. It is one thing, in the very presence of the beloved, to withdraw attention from his beauty, and frigidly drag in that of the sun and moon and flowers; and another thing, in his absence, to make all beautiful things in nature mere types and memorials of his beauty. This is a distinction which seems peculiar to Shakespeare. Petrarch has made little difference between his present and his absent mistress in regard to the similitudes with which he compliments her. He tells her to her face that if she died, and her soul were placed between the earth and sun, the sun's light would be dimmed by the contrast (Son. 18). When Laura goes the sky puts on mourning (Son. 26); when she comes back she makes fine weather (Son. 27). She is a conqueror's laurel, and so forth. Spenser erred like Petrarch in this particular. He makes the stars as it were a necklace, the sun itself a foil, and heaven a mere robe and ornament for his mistress. She contains all the earth's riches (Son. 15); her eyes are sapphires, her lips rubies, her teeth pearls, her forehead ivory, her hair gold, her hands silver, her smile sunshine (Son. 40), her fragrance that of April flowers (Son. 64), her eyes brighter than sun, moon, stars, fire, lightning, diamond, crystal, and glass, and most like the Maker's self. From all this artificial conventionality Shakespeare separates himself.

> So is it not with me, as with that Muse
> Stirred by a painted beauty to his verse
> Who heaven himself as ornament doth use.

"Painted beauty" means simply "a woman," and refers to the "artificial handsomeness" which was in fashion late in Elizabeth's reign. The Queen "never saw herself in a true glass after she became old," as Jonson told Drummond: "they painted her, and sometimes would vermilion her nose." Hamlet (in the Quartos) says to Ophelia about her sex, "I have heard of your paintings too: God hath given you one face, and you make yourselves another." In the folio of 1623 "painting" becomes "prattling," and "face" "pace." Perhaps face-painting went out of fashion after the old Queen's death. But at the date of these Sonnets false faces and false hair were the rule, as we may see by Sonnets 68, 69, and 127. Shakespeare makes farther invectives against the practice in *Love's Labour's Lost*, *The Merchant of Venice*, and *Timon of Athens*. Hall also satirizes it, and Harrington has an epigram upon it. Shakespeare's indignation with rouge and wigs was the outward form of his inmost hatred of mere conventionalities—

> Taffata phrases, silken terms precise,
> Three-piled hyperboles, spruce affectation, . . .
> Figures pedantical,

and of his artistic feeling that in the presence of a great passion all pedantry is out of place. The concentrated purpose wipes away from the memory

> all trivial fond records,
> All saws of books, all forms, all pressures past
> That youth and observation copied there.

He hates the use of the rouge-pot as much for poetry as for the face.

The next Sonnet (22) turns upon another common-place of sonnet philosophy:—

> All that beauty that doth cover thee
> Is but the seemly raiment of my heart,
> Which in thy breast doth live, as thine in me.

This Sonnet must be taken in connection with the 24th: together they show that in this stage of love the heart is only enamoured of beauty's external form. The reciprocal admiration of each lover for the other's beauty, though it seems to effect that interchange of heart which is only fully possible in perfected love, yet does it in a very superficial way. "Fancy" is still in its cradle; it has not yet been delivered from the thraldom of the eyes; and eyes "draw but what they see, know not the heart." The intermediate Sonnet (23) turns upon another commonplace of the philosophy—the awe and trouble which possesses the lover and makes him tongue-tied in the presence of his friend. This trembling, prescribed by the Codex Amoris, is spoken of in the 4th, 5th, 6th, and 7th Sonnets of Dante's *Vita Nuova*, and in several of Petrarch's, as Sonnet 34, where he says that in Laura's presence he can neither speak, nor cry, nor sigh; and that when his tongue would ask recompense, it is frozen, and its words are imperfect, like a dreamer's. Similarly Shakespeare says that the friend is not to believe his ears, but his eyes are to read "what silent love hath writ;" for "to hear with eyes belongs to love's fine wit." These Sonnets are clearly descriptive of the various phases of love entering by the eyes. The 25th Sonnet sums up the happiness of this love: court favourites live in the royal eye, and die of a frown. It is only the perpetual and present smile of fortune that maintains the warrior's fame. But

> Happy I, that love and am beloved
> Where I may not remove, nor be removed.

With the 26th Sonnet we enter the second degree of the scale of love. Love now learns through absence to be independent of the eyes. This second part begins with a "written embassage," the dedicatory nature of which is so clear that Mr. Gerald Massey has wrenched it from its proper place to make it the preface to all the Sonnets. It is the introduction to the poems of absence. The lover will not venture to show himself in his friend's presence till his "bare" verses are clothed with his friend's loving favour—

> Then may I dare to boast how I do love thee:
> Till then, not show my head where thou may'st prove me.

In its reference to the imperfect utterance of the poet's pen, this Sonnet clearly refers back to Sonnet 23. There he said that his verses expressed his thoughts better than his words could do; here, that these verses are bare till the friend takes them and meditates on them alone, and by his favour "puts apparel" on their tattered love. The 27th and 28th Sonnets depict the first miseries of absence; but through this wretchedness the "shadow" of the friend shines, brightening the day, and gilding the night—for already the first effect of absence upon the imagination is to mitigate the realism of Sonnet 21, which abjures all hyperbole. In Sonnet 29, perhaps the most exquisite of the series, the remembrance of the friend's sweet love is made the one antidote for all the sorrows of life; in Sonnets 30 and 31, again, it becomes the substitute for all past and vanished loves—a kind of new life in which "all losses are restored," and the images of dead friends revivified. Sonnet 32 closes this little series, which begins with Sonnet 26, with a kind of repetition and enlargement of the opening motive. In one place the poet says to his friend, "think over my verses in my absence;" in the other, "think over them when I am dead, and supply their defects by your kind thoughts." In the gradual progress of love we shall find that the poet once more reverts to this thought (in Sonnet 71), and begs his friend to forget him and his poetry alike after death, if the remembrance brings pain. Another little series of Sonnets begins with the 33rd, when the unkind thoughts which besiege the absent begin to make their appearance. In Sonnet 33 the lover doubts of his friend's constancy:—

> He was but one hour mine,
> The region cloud hath masked him from me now.

In the 34th the lover endures some disgrace at his friend's

hands. But in the 35th he declares that no doubts or disgraces can touch his love, and that he even makes himself an accessory to his friend's misdeeds by excusing them. Then, from the notion that the accessory is equally worthy of blame with the principal, he concludes, in Sonnet 36, that absence must be perpetual; he cannot ask his friend to return to one whose bad name he would have to share. As his friend is identified with him, so also his friend's good report becomes his personal concern; and this, with his unworthiness, can only be maintained by separation. And separation has its own consolations. Even the report of his friend's glory, the shadow of his beauty, birth, wealth, and wit, gives him substantial comfort (Sonnet 37). He feels himself blessed when he knows his friend is blessed—

> Look, what is best, that best I wish in thee,
> This wish I have; then ten times happy me!

It is characteristic of this early stage in the ladder of love that all the qualities on which it dwells are such as are more or less external. In the first stage, love is taken in through the eyes, and is kindled only by beauty; in the second, it enters through the sensible imagination, and is kindled by the qualities which affect this imagination—not only beauty, but rank, wealth, and wit.

The third stage in the scale begins with Sonnet 38. Like the 26th, it is a dedicatory and introductory sonnet. The poet declares that whatever excellence appears in his poems is all due to the inspiration they derive from his friend, who is the tenth Muse—

> O give thyself the thanks if aught in me
> Worthy perusal stand against thy sight.

The third stage of love idealizes the data of imagination, and gathers them all up in the friend, in whom the lover lives a second life; so that, as Crescimbeni says, "he has gained, not one but two lives." With this idea Shakespeare, in Sonnet 39, moralizes on the benefits of absence, which teaches "how to make one twain," to dissolve one life into two, as well as to combine two into one. Then follow three Sonnets which have been a stumbling-block to all interpreters. Taken in connection with Sonnets 133, 134, the Sonnets 40–42 clearly tell a disgraceful story. The lover has some mistress, a married woman, with whom he has a guilty intimacy. He uses his friend as a go-between, and his friend supplants him. Interpreted biographically of the poet and his friend, the story is shocking. It is also improbable in the highest degree that the man who maintains so dignified a silence about himself, or who, when he does speak, as in Sonnet 121, asserts so clearly his own superiority to vulgar scandal, should have only lifted the veil to let us behold such a disgrace as this. On the other hand, Mr. Massey's interpretation, which makes Elizabeth Vernon the speaker and Lady Rich the person addressed, however ingenious in its combinations and successful in upholding Shakespeare's dignity, can only itself be upheld by destroying the whole internal organization of the Sonnets, and in some of them by literally making black into white. But in our theory they fall most naturally into place. The love of the friends has to be tried by jealousy, but in this stage of love the jealousy which suspects a preference for another friend would be premature; its place is found in the stage of ideal love. Here we require the more superficial jealousy, which would keep to itself those special gifts of the friend which kindle the lover's fancy. Now the lover could not be jealous of his friend's wife; he has devoted seventeen sonnets to one theme, an invitation to him to marry. He could not be jealous of his friend's mistress; in Sonnet 20 he has expressly left him free in his relations with women;—"Mine be thy love, and thy love's use their treasure." He could not be jealous of his friend's friend; for this jealousy belongs to a higher stage of love, that ideal love which admits of no plurality in affection, and which, as Sonnet 119 shows, cancels also the freedom with respect to women which Sonnet 20 grants. The poet must, therefore, devise some real cause for jealousy, and this he has done in the manner we have indicated. In Sonnets 33, 34 he merely alludes to this theft, to blame it, to forgive it, and to excuse it. He owns in Sonnet 35 that the excuse he makes for it is disgraceful in itself, and in Sonnet 36 that it is quite reason enough why his friend should remain separate from him. In Sonnet 40 he refers more explicitly to the transaction, and declares that it must not make him and his friend into foes; in Sonnet 41 he again excuses it, and in Sonnet 42 he even finds in it a fresh symptom of love—

> But here's the joy—my friend and I are one;
> Sweet flattery! then she loves but me alone.

The conclusion is not moral; but the imaginative stage of love is not yet moral. It is as yet but a sentimental fancy; and the scale of love shows by what stages this sentimental fancy is gradually transformed from a non-moral into a moral affection. On the other hand, it must be remembered that all the stages in the scale of love are symmetrical; the earlier foreshadow the later. And a general formula which may be quite immoral in a lower application may represent true morality in a higher one. Mr. Gerald Massey's interpretation saves Shakespeare's reputation; but these Sonnets are capable of a better vindication. The highest *amor amicitiæ* of which man is capable is directed to God. Now any one who reads Sonnets 40-42 will see that they are as applicable as the Song of Solomon itself to the stage of divine Love. If God deprives a man of an object of earthly affection, either by taking it to Himself or by raising in it an affection to Him which supplants and extinguishes all human loves, the only permissible feeling in man is that which Shakespeare formulates in these three Sonnets. They contain a genuine and unassailable analysis of love, though the disagreeable nature of their first and obvious meaning rather tempts the common observer to neglect examining the real depth of their truth and beauty.

This stage of love ends with a short series of three Sonnets, 43-45, which bring to light the unsatisfactory nature of this merely imaginary love. It is shadowy and unsubstantial. It does not attain to the deep recesses of the soul; it lives rather in the imagination and senses, which are tied to the four material elements of which the body is composed, than in the nimble thought to which distance is nothing, and bodily presence or absence is all one. With this transitional reflection the first division of the first great series of Sonnets is brought to a close. Shakespeare has shown us the three steps of love, conceived in the eyes, generalized in the imagination, and again concentrated in the judgment, but not yet idealized—not yet possessing the whole heart.

To recapitulate. The first stage of love is represented

in Sonnets 1 to 25. In the first twenty the lover is represented gradually coming nearer to his object, beginning with a distant respect, and ending with a close intimacy. Then Sonnets 21 to 25 express the first unity of love's simple apprehension, in which it confounds the two lovers into one. The second stage is shown in Sonnets 26 to 37. Here this unity is put through its trials. It is not troubled by the duality of absence (26–28) nor by difference of station, nor by private sorrows (29). It envelopes and "sublates," as an Hegelian would say, all former loves, restoring them in a different form, and raising them to a new life (30, 31). It expects to survive death (32); it excuses all offences, reckoning them as self-inflicted wounds, and making the sufferer an accessory to the offender (33–35); hence it cries, "depart from me for I am a sinful man," and shows how absence conduces to the growth of love (35–37). The third stage is exhibited in Sonnets 38 to 45. Love not only ceases to be troubled by the trials which it surmounts in the second stage; it even assimilates them, and turns them into its own essence. Absence becomes the dualistic life of love, and proves that it is expedient that friends should live divided (39); jealousy itself becomes a reunion of this dualism, and a fresh proof that "my friend and I are one" (40—42); and the very insufficiency of the materialistic elements of these first stages of love becomes a force which suggests and helps to carry out the transformation of an imaginative into an ideal love (43—45).

CHAPTER VI.

IDEAL LOVE IN THE SONNETS.

IMAGINATIVE love occupies the three lower grades in the scale, and ideal love the three higher. Ideal love begins with the substitution of intellectual for sensible beauty; for if love is born in the eyes, its life is in the mind. This change is indicated by Shakespeare in Sonnets 46 and 47. What the eye has been to the prior stages of love, the heart is now to be for the later. As before, the eye "played the painter, and engraved the form of beauty on the heart's tablets" (Sonnet 24)—so now, the heart is to play the painter, and to interpret the friend's heart to the lover's consciousness. To know another man, says Hamlet, is to know one's self. Love therefore when transferred from the beauty of form to that of the mind depends upon the knowledge of one's self; for this knowledge is our grammar and dictionary whereby we may interpret the tokens which reveal to us the hearts and minds of others. Shakespeare then, after introducing the subject in Sonnets 46, 47, has to show how love acquires, of itself, this self-knowledge. First he recurs to the general topic of absence, which leads the lover to fear that absence only typifies the entire loss of his friend (Son. 48). Then he asks himself—"but what claim have I to keep him?" This leads him to a "knowledge of his own desert," and to the confession that he "can allege no cause" why he should be loved (Son. 49). The two next Sonnets (50 and 51) should be compared with Petrarch's "Io mi rivolgo indietro a ciascun passo." The intention is to show how much ideal love transcends the animal powers. The "dull flesh," "the beast that bears" the man, appears in its slowness to sympathize with him in the pains of absence; but in the ardour of desire, and in the triumph of return, the soul must be its own vehicle; no flesh can keep abreast of the mind in its "fiery race," and therefore all such weak auxiliaries have "leave to go." Sonnet 52 carries this asceticism of love even further, and dispenses, except on rare occasions, even with the imagination of the friend's shape. Every object reminds the lover of his friend's beauty (53), but nothing can represent his "constant heart." And yet (54) it is not the visible beauty, but the constant heart or invisible truth, which gives a man his worth. This truth, therefore, and no longer the mere outward form, as in Sonnet 5, the poet's verse is henceforth to distil, to make its memory live for ever (55) and "dwell in lovers' eyes."

With Sonnet 56 a new vein of feeling comes in. The poet finds that the abstention and asceticism of the last few sonnets only "kills the spirit of love by a perpetual dulness." He once more therefore gives play to his imagination. He thinks of the bodily presence of his friend; he wonders where he is and what he is doing, and checks his rising suspicions by the deepest self-humiliation. Being his friend's slave, how can he demand an account of what he is doing? (Sonnets 57, 58). He finds it much more to the purpose to search old records to find his friend's "image in some antique book," written "since mind at first in character was done" (59). Thus love retires into itself, chews the cud of meditation, and bears again "the second burden of a former child" by remodelling its old thoughts, and giving new birth to pre-existing ideas. Such new birth is altogether of a higher character than natural nativity, which "crawls to maturity" and is eclipsed. The new life which the poet promises to confer on his friend is one that "shall stand to times in hope" (60).

In Sonnet 61 the poet asks whether his friend's image which visits him so often is sent by him, or is conjured up by his own love. It is, he replies, his own love. But if he creates the image, what must be his own worth that is capable of casting such a shadow? All former self-inspection ended in self-abasement; this ends in a very different self-appreciation (62):—

> Methinks no face so gracious is as mine,
> No shape so true, no truth of such account;
> And for myself mine own worth do define,
> As I all other in all worths surmount.

And though he refers all this excellence to his friend, his second self, yet it remains true that he must have all its elements in his own person, or he would not be able to comprehend it. In himself, however, the excellence only exists "crushed and o'erworn by Time." But as beauty still exists even in his wrinkles, so he will take care that his friend's beauty shall live in the "black lines" which his pen traces; and these lines shall defy Time, after the beauty which they celebrate has long been laid in the dust (63–65).

The main features of this stage of ideal love are the three self-inspections whereby the lover comes to the knowledge of his own heart. First, he recognizes its absolute worthlessness by its defects; secondly, he determines its relation to the friend, whose slave and vassal he feels himself to be; and thirdly, he recognizes its real nobility when he finds in it those principles of superlative excellence which his modesty will not allow him to attribute to himself. Henceforth the self-conscious heart, and not the sensuous imagination, becomes the true interpreter of love.

When once, through self-inspection, the lover has become acquainted with his own soul, and therein with souls in general, he is perforce obliged to substitute a spiritual beauty for the material beauty which he has hitherto worshipped. And this substitution indicates an advance of the understanding from the concrete to the abstract. The lover, says Plato, has now no eyes for gold or colours or outward beauties, but only for the beauty of souls, of arts, of sciences, and of institutions. He is no longer distressed by the waning of fair faces, or the fading of flowers, but by the soul which does not fulfil its high promises, by art which misses its aim, by science which babbles, by political institutions which are turned to purposes of oppression and revolutionary destruction, and by a religion which forswears its faith. To this new phase of love Sonnet 66 is an introduction as beautiful as it is appropriate. In common with Hamlet's famous soliloquy, and indeed in harmony with all Shakespeare's later tragedies, it expresses the poet's deep disgust with the world, and society as he saw them, and declares that his ideal love was the only thing which made life tolerable to him. But why, he asks in Sonnets 67, 68, should this love continue alive amidst the impiety and falsehood of the age? In order, he replies, "To show false art what beauty was of yore." Again, why, he asks in Sonnets 69, 70, should this love live in a world which only slanders it? Slander, he replies, is inevitable when an ideal principle manifests itself in action; men will construe this action after their own fashion.

> They look into the beauty of thy mind,
> And that, in guess, they measure by thy deeds.

And thus slander simply approves worth. Sonnet 70 goes far to prove the purely philosophical character of the whole series. While the love was simply imaginative, and contemplated only an outward beauty, it was possible to attribute all kinds of "sensual faults" (Son. 35) to the "lascivious grace" of the friend. Now, however, that the friend has become a type of ideal beauty, it is necessary to say of him—

> —Thou present'st a pure unstained prime;
> Thou hast pass'd by the ambush of young days,
> Either not assailed, or victor being charged.

In the two next Sonnets (71, 72) the lover with most intense feeling begs the friend to forget him and his verses after death, "if thinking on me then should make you woe." And in the two next he dwells on the short space yet left to him, which at once makes his friend's love more strong "To love that well which thou must leave ere long," and urges the poet to pour out his whole spirit into the verses which he consecrates to his friend's immortality. Mr. Carlyle sees in Shakespeare the "sovereign poet who was sent to take note of" the passing forms of chivalry and mediæval Catholicism. In these Sonnets he really seems to feel himself to be the last minstrel and only herald of a beauty that was already out of date. But he has a supreme confidence in his cause, and a confidence mingled with diffidence in his own powers. Hence his unwillingness to link his love so indissolubly to himself as to make it perish with him. Hence too, mingled with his yearnings for death and oblivion, his confidence that his cause will be immortalized in his verse. He seems to feel that he is destined to a temporary oblivion, but that afterwards his memory will revive, and his writings will become a power to perpetuate the ideals which they embody.

The next two Sonnets, 75, 76, record his single attachment to his ideal love. Absent or present, it is the sole food of his thoughts, and the only topic of his monotonous verse. In Sonnet 77 he gives his friend a note book, and entreats him to commit his thoughts, the children of his brain, to its waste blanks. As imaginative love began with beseeching the friend to marry and leave children like himself, so ideal love looks for offspring—not, however, of the body, but of the mind. The poet felt that the life of the world was changing. He held up a mirror to the old life, that it might paint itself and put itself upon record. In this record the old life lies not dead, but as it were in a nurse's arms, in order once more to rise, and "to take a new acquaintance" of the mind of man. The Sonnet reads to this effect:—"Literature is the mirror and the dial of the ebb and flow in the development of mankind; it registers the changes of ideas and the lapse of ages. Take off then the reflection of the present waning age; transfer it to your paper; commit it to the world; it will come to light in due time, and serve the purposes of progress." For all advance rests on what is already secured; the future is built on the present, as the present on the past.

After this, the purport of the next nine Sonnets, on jealousy, will be clear. Whether any other poet, Marlowe, or Drayton, or Daniel, or Spenser, really usurped Shakespeare's place in the affections of W. H. cannot be determined from them. The course of the argument requires here that ideal love should be tried by an ideal and intellectual jealousy, as imaginative love was tried by an imaginative jealousy in Sonnets 40-42. The poet, fresh from lamenting the transient stay of the beauty he loved, and from proposing it as the model for future ages, to be preserved in the truth-telling records of unaffected verse, naturally is indignant that the subject should be appropriated by men of the affected school whose "gross painting" and "strained touches of rhetoric" only distort the truth they pretend to describe. The lover's object is to think true thoughts, not to speak fine words. To him, the presence of the ideal love in the heart and mind supplies for all lack of education and skill. He has not to ransack the universe for comparisons, but has only to copy what he sees in his ideal love—none can say more

> Than this rich praise, that you alone are you. (Son. 84.)

Such creation is the highest aim of art. It gives to its object an individuality which serves to make it for ever unique.

In the next series of Sonnets, 87-96, Love seems to yield to jealousy. The rival has prevailed, and the lover relinquishes his claims on his friend's heart. As in a previous Sonnet, he attributes this breach to his own unworthiness. Yet the self-depreciation here has an additional element. In Sonnet 49 it was simply a result of a comparison of himself, as known by self-reflection, to his ideal love. Jealousy gives rise in the lover to a self-depreciation in comparison with a third person. The first was a mere act of self-apprehension; the second is an act of self-judgment. Such self-judgment the lover practises in Sonnets 87-96. The legal phraseology of Sonnet 87 is itself suggestive of the process of judgment. In the next, the poet excuses his friend's lack of love by a confession of his own secret faults, like that which Hamlet makes to Ophelia. He owns beforehand

> Thou canst not, love, disgrace me half so ill
> As I'll myself disgrace. (Son. 89.)

But he asks that, if he is to be disgraced, it may be at once; that the threatened evil may not perpetually hang over him (90). This is the only bitterness in his cup—

> Wretched in this alone that thou may'st take
> All this [thy love] away, and me most wretched make. (Son. 91.)

Yet it cannot effectually be taken away. For such a loss would be death; and death is unconscious. If the friend is false, the lover will never know it (92, 93). Then the lover almost accepts the hypothesis of the friend's falsehood. His rose has not only colour to please the eyes, but the spiritual fragrance which captivates the mind; but what if this sweetness "with base infection meet"?

> For sweetest things turn sourest by their deeds:
> Lilies that fester smell far worse than weeds (Son. 94.)

So he concludes by warning his friend that though his

beauty covers every blot, yet in time "the hardest knife loses its edge" (95.) Thus the second stage of ideal love ends with a negative operation of the judgment, which seems to threaten the very existence of love. It is to be noticed that Sonnet 96, the last in the second stage of ideal love, ends with the same couplet as Sonnet 36, the last but one in the second stage of imaginative love. For the same situations recur, but ever in a higher significance.

In the third stage of ideal love all the negations of the judgment are rectified, and its scattered premisses drawn up into one conclusion. The universal soul, the "sacred universal love," which is the final object of ideal love, contains in itself, in a transcendant sense, all that was found in the lower grades of love. Hence this stage is fitly introduced with three beautiful Sonnets, which, in thorough contradiction with Sonnet 21, disparage all the bright lamps of the universe in comparison with the beauty of the friend. For though it is folly to compare a handsome face to sun, and moon, and stars, it is, on the other hand, true that a soul is, in its own nature, better than all the inanimate world, and a spiritual beauty above all possible corporeal beauty. These three Sonnets should be compared with a beautiful and well-known passage in S. Augustine's Confessions (x. 8). The identity of words and imagery in the two writers will suggest an identity in their meaning. Then, in Sonnets 100, 101, the poet rebukes his muse for her silence. Though her song cannot improve beauty, it can immortalize it. In the next two Sonnets, 102, 103, he excuses silence. It is not becoming to merchandize love in the hubbub of the world's mart, and his verse only mars that which it cannot mend. In Sonnet 104 he declares that his love has passed through its three great seasons, and in 105 that it has united the three elements of love—beauty, goodness, and truth—into a single whole—" one, still such, and ever so."

> Fair, kind, and true have often lived alone,
> Which three till now never kept seat in one.

For the final stage of love is the synthesis of all its elements. To describe it the poet takes from old literature all the notes that he can find of beauty, and uses them as if they had been prophecies prefiguring his present love (106), but neither his own fears nor these prophetic foreshadowings can set limits to his love. The moon, after eclipses which augurs have declared deadly, reappears; and his love shall live in his verses (107). Day by day he will repeat the same *paternoster* of love; for age kills it not (108), but rather gives it new life.

The lover's suspicions and apparent falseness, the fickleness of his affections, the misfortunes of his life, and the scandal which surrounds his name, are all made into fuel for all-consuming, all-embracing love in Sonnets 109–112. The two next sonnets describe the idealizing of the imagination—turning the eye into mind, and the mind into an eye that creates out of chaotic masses images of ideal beauty. In Sonnet 115 the poet corrects former sonnets, such as 76, 105, 107, which seem to say "now I love you best," as if the lover feared for the future of his love, instead of remembering that love is a babe that grows continually, and that growth is the condition of love as it is of life. In the next Sonnet, 116, he celebrates love as the marriage of true minds, a union far above alteration or motion, guiding life, like a star in the heavens. In the next series of four sonnets (117–120), all the moral aberrations of both the lover and friend are first condemned and then consumed in the furnace of love, in order to make its flame the hotter. Better is made still better even by evil; when once the tide turns, and the flow of improvement sets in, everything works with it, and even contradictions and aberrations contribute to the one great conclusion— for all discords are resolved in the final concord. The true nature of evil is, however, distinctly allowed, and the soul of goodness which it contains is made to consist not in anything intrinsic to evil, but in the reaction which it causes. Evil is a kind of analytic power, which prepares for the great synthetic process of perfected love. After the touching confession of evil and its uses, the lover proceeds to state the paradox (121) that it is better to be evil than to be thought so. The reaction from evil produces good under the organizing and healing influence of love. But the evil report chases away love, and with it the hope of perfection. The lover therefore asserts in the strongest way his own rectitude; in Sonnet 122 he defends himself for the seeming carelessness of giving away the table-book which in Sonnet 77 he had given to his friend, and which had been returned to him full of notes. His memory needed no such reminders of his friend—

> To keep an adjunct to remember thee
> Were to import forgetfulness in me.

Unkindness is turned into kindness, and carelessness becomes a sign of careful memory. In Sonnet 123 he defies Time and his registers; his love has the character of eternity, and is not helped by any temporal records. In Sonnet 124 he enlarges on the eternal character of his love. It is not the child of state, varying with fortune. It depends not on the accidents of smiling pomp or thralled discontent. It fears not the heretic policy which prefers the temporal to the eternal, but proves itself altogether politic by showing itself invincible and unchangeable. It seeks not (125) external honours, and refuses to base its claims to immortality on favour and form. But its highest act is one of sacrifice:—

> —take thou my oblation, poor but free,
> Which is not mixed with seconds, knows no art
> But mutual render, only me for thee.

As he had used the language of the Lord's Prayer in Sonnet 108, so here he uses the language of an act still more solemn than prayer, the oblation of the Eucharist. The external ceremony is but the offering of a piece of wastel bread; the internal effect is that two hearts, the lover and the ideal love, mingle together, and mutually give themselves to each other. Then, as if the poet remembered that this was a rite of a proscribed religion, he concludes with the exclamation—

> Hence, thou suborned informer; a true soul,
> When most impeached, stands least in thy control.

Sonnet 126 is imperfect in form, and though belonging to the series in its general tone, has no special place therein, and hence is appended as a mere tag to it. That it was placed here, and not at the end of all the Sonnets, is a farther proof that the whole first series down to this place have for their object the "lovely boy" who is so rarely alluded to distinctly after Sonnet 27 that Mr. Gerald

IDEAL LOVE IN THE SONNETS.

Massey thinks himself entitled to consider most of the intermediate Sonnets to be addressed to women. The true reason why sex is not mentioned is that in the gradual elevation of love, and in its transformations through successive stages, its object becomes more and more generalized, more spiritual, with less definite sex, or definite human personality. This consideration does not absolutely preclude reference to the "sweet boy," even in so late and religiously toned a sonnet as 108. But it is quite reason enough to account for the sudden cessation of the continuous reference to the manhood and personality of the beloved object after Sonnet 27, when it will be remembered imaginative love is just entering on its second phase of abstraction and analysis.

In this brief sketch of the connection of these sonnets, and of their agreement with the acknowledged philosophy of other sonnet writers, it has been manifestly impossible to do more than trace their leading ideas, the thread of connection which binds them together, and makes them into a consistent series. This thread is often concealed by the variety and splendour of the jewels that are strung upon it; the philosophic poet covers the bare skeleton which we have traced with the most exuberant tissues, with a profusion of thought and images which is simply astonishing. But under all this wealth the main outline of the pre-existing idea which was part of the current Platonism of the epoch may be traced, if not easily, at least with precision and certainty.

CHAPTER VII.

VULGAR LOVE IN THE SONNETS.

In the second series of Sonnets Shakespeare represents the progress of the "love of despair." As the beauty which corresponds to the higher love finds its fitting symbol in the "man right fair" of the former series, so the beauty which corresponds to the lower love is betokened in the second series by a gypsy-like woman, with black eyes and hair, and a complexion "coloured ill." The poet represents this love not as an original and natural feeling, but as a sentiment arising from the disappointment of higher aspirations. First, the lover who looks for true beauty cannot find it, but only its counterfeits (Son. 127), and so in his despair he surrenders himself to the black eyes which do not pretend to possess the true beauty, but by their very contradiction to it become its most eloquent representatives. By the side of this beauty the lover stands, resigning himself to its attractions (128), clearly knowing to what a hell it is leading him, but unable to conquer its temptations (129), appreciating its real deficiencies, but confessing its mysterious power over him (130). Secondly, in absence "by himself alone," "thinking on his mistress's face," he wonders how her blackness can seem fair to him; and he concludes that it is only in her deeds, not in her face, that she is black (131); or that if she is black, it is only in mourning for his pain (132); and this compassion of hers makes her beautiful in his eyes. Thirdly, his own fancy is strengthened by his friend's judgment. His friend has carried messages to and from his mistress, and has ended by supplanting him. The friend's fancy therefore has been caught by the hooks that captivated the poet, whose judgment is thus confirmed by another's (133, 134). And these three steps complete the imaginative stage of sensual love.

The ideal stage of this lower love begins with Sonnet 135. In the previous sonnet the poet had confessed to his mistress that "he [the friend] is thine, and I myself mortgaged to thy will"—"thou hast both him and me." First, then, he tells her "thou hast thy will, and Will to boot, and Will in overplus," confounding by a verbal quibble his own and perhaps his friend's name Will with his mistress's volition, and aiming no longer at her beauty, but at her consent and her kindness, even though her kindness was that of an abandoned woman. For as his imagination had overpowered his eyes, so his corrupt partiality had overpowered his heart's judgment, and made it "think that a several plot" which it knew to be "the wide world's common place" (137). It is possible that as Shakespeare drew largely on Sidney, who was called "Willy" by his friends, these later sonnets, intended to illustrate the progress of lawless love, are purposely made to suggest Sidney's notorious intrigues with his "Stella," Lady Rich, and to be a kind of translation into their real meaning of the famous sonnets which he dedicated to her. Secondly, having thus idealized corrupt love, and given it its bias towards a vicious indulgence, the next step is to make its vices bear the semblance of virtues. Its falsehood becomes truth (138), its inconstancy kindness (139), and hypocrisy its life (140); its folly becomes its torment, and therefore in some sense its atonement (141); its sinful loves and virtuous hates become thoroughly confused (142), and the lover finally contents himself with the mere dregs of his mistress's love; asking only that he may have his will with her, because she has her will with others; and thus setting up inconstancy as the ideal qualification of the lower love (143): for communism in morals, scepticism in philosophy, and pantheism in religion are the idealizations of the "love of despair." And thirdly, the last stage of the lower love in its ideal state exhibits the real incompatibility between it and the higher love. In their imaginative states the two kinds of love can coexist, as we see in Sonnets 40, 41, compared with 133–135. Now, however, "the female evil tempteth the better angel from" the lover's side, and "would corrupt his saint to be a devil" (144). But the man who abandons the higher love prefers to be dependent on his "female evil's" unkind kindness (145), though it leads him to all sorts of outward luxury, to pamper his body and starve his soul (146). This love conducts its victim to frantic, and at the same time conscious, madness—

> For I have sworn thee fair, and thought thee bright,
> Who art as black as hell, as dark as night—(147)—

to voluntary blindness (148), to a complete and fawning submission of his acts and sentiments to his mistress's caprices (149); to an abeyance of reason, which loves the more, the more it sees just cause of hate (150), to a half-playful, half-serious devotion of conscience even to the most brutal enjoyments (151); and to the loss of all honesty through devotion to one whose kindness, love, truth, and constancy he had defended while he knew them to be utterly incapable of defence (152).

Thus it will be seen that both series of sonnets go regularly through all the steps of the scale of love; and in each, the corresponding step is treated in an analogous way. As the first series begins with the earnest desire to see the beauty of the beloved one immortalize itself in offspring, so the second begins with declaring that beauty is dead, and its offspring bastard. This despair for the future of beauty is naturally connected with the immorality of this lower love—with the "murderous, bloody, savage, rude, cruel" nature ascribed to it in Sonnet 124. Mr. Gerald Massey wishes to prove that as the "mourning eyes" of the mistress in these sonnets are clearly borrowed from Sidney's Sonnets to Stella, the same woman, Penelope Rich, was their heroine also; and he takes great pains to identify the "black wires" which grew on the head of Shakespeare's gypsy with the golden locks which Sidney sings. It would have been more to the purpose to refer to Shakespeare's own conception of black-eyed women in his dramas. Biron in *Love's Labour's Lost* talks of his mistress's eyes and hair mourning for the false hair and complexion which women put on—just as the lover speaks in Sonnet 127; and in Shakespeare's earliest play, *Titus Andronicus*, he had made Aaron say that the only face which needs no paint is the black one—

> Coal black is better than another hue,
> In that it scorns to bear another hue.

Thus, for certain purposes a gypsy face, like Cleopatra's, became the new fashion of a beauty which represented not hope, but despair—not the reproductiveness of "fairest creatures," but the mourning retrospect of a barren regret, solacing itself with present licence. The idea of Sonnet 128 is borrowed by Ben Jonson, *Every Man out of his Humour*, iii. 3, where Fastidious Brisk says of his lady and her lute, "You see the subject of her sweet fingers there. Oh, she tickles it so that she makes it laugh most divinely. . . . I have wished myself to be that instrument a thousand times." The thought of Sonnet 129 is found in another early play of Shakespeare's—*Pericles*:

> One sin, I know, another doth provoke:
> Murder's as near to lust as flame to smoke.
> Poison and treason are the hands of sin.

It is to be noticed that the two most directly religious sonnets (129 and 146) occur in the second series. For remorse of conscience holds the same place in the lower love as criminal passions in the higher. As such passions are obstacles to the progress of a pure love, so sorrow for them, and purposes of amendment, are obstacles to the progress of a guilty love. Again, it will be noticed that in the imaginative stage of this lower love, conscience protests against the animal passions only; whereas in its ideal stage conscience has to protest in general against the care lavished on the body at the expense of the soul. For as the higher love, when idealized, expands into political virtues, so does the lower love, when idealized, ramify into every "lust of the eye, and pride of life." Sonnet 146 reminds one of Sidney's last sonnet—

> Leave me, O Love, which reachest but to dust;
> And thou, my mind, aspire to higher things.
> Grow rich in that which never taketh rust:
> Whatever fades but fading pleasure brings.

And its phraseology seems imitated from the close of Chaucer's Canterbury Tales: "This blisful regne may men purchace by poverte espirituel, and the glorie by lowenesse, the plente of joye by hunger and thurst, and reste by travaile, and the lif by deth and mortificacioun of synne."

Some of these later sonnets find their parallels, as we have seen, in some of Shakespeare's earliest dramas; others find them in his latest plays. Thus, with Sonnet 147 we may compare Coriolanus's speech to the mob—

> Your affections are
> A sick man's appetite, who desires that most
> Which would increase his evil.

While Sonnet 149 finds a curiously exact parallel in a speech of Catherine in *King Henry VIII.*, ii., 4, 29—

> Which of your friends
> Have I not strove to love, although I knew
> He were mine enemy? What friend of mine
> That had to him derived your anger, did I
> Continue in my liking? Nay, gave notice
> He was from thence discharged.

Perhaps these, and several other parallelisms which might be produced, may be taken as an indication that the composition of the sonnets was continued over a long period of time, and that the order of their arrangement was not the order of their composition. But as they were all meant to illustrate some special phase in a well-known philosophical system, they would all naturally fall into place, and it would be an easy task for the poet to give them their true arrangement.

CHAPTER VIII.

CONCLUSION.

THE question now once more arises, how far these Sonnets are to be considered autobiographical. It may be at once conceded that they paint the poet's ideas and character; that they give us a good notion of what his sentiments would have been in given situations. But the situations themselves, are they imaginary, or are they real? Are they merely dramatic devices to serve as framework for the sentiments, or are they historically true? Can we receive Sonnets 40-42, 133, 134 as true histories of the poet, his friend, and their common mistress? If so, we should have still to explain the directly contradictory statements in Sonnets 70, 79, and 121. It is, therefore, much more natural to take the framework of the Sonnets as a mere imagination, devised to display the progress of love to the best advantage. But if the great outlines are imaginary, still multitudes of the details may be true. The sentiments and opinions are the writer's own actual thoughts, and they may hold in solution many a true statement of the facts of his life. It would be easy to say that whatever detail is necessary for the development of the theme may be classed among the inventions of the poet; while whatever is not so necessary is probably founded on fact. But the application of such a test would be entirely uncertain. / For instance, talking of his own death in Sonnet 74, the poet calls his dead body "the coward conquest of a wretch's knife." Had he been stabbed, and did he write this sonnet while his life was in danger? Again, in Sonnet 37 he says, "I, made lame by Fortune's dearest spite;" and in Sonnet 89, "Speak of my lameness, and I straight will halt." Are we to conclude that he was really lame? Again, there are many indications of time in the sonnets. In Sonnet 2 he fixes on the age of forty as that which digs deep trenches in beauty's field. In Sonnet 62 he calls himself "beated and chopped with tann'd antiquity." In Sonnet 73 he has reached the autumn and twilight of life; that is, he is at least forty years old. But on the other hand when, after an absence during summer and autumn (97) and a spring (98) from his friend, he renews his poetical exercises, he declares (104) that it is three years since he first knew him. Now as Shakespeare was born in 1564, he was forty years old in 1604, and his sonnets should have begun some three years before—about 1600. Yet they were handed about in MS. before 1598. If the W. H. of Thorpe's dedication is the Earl of Southampton, or if he was the "friend" of the first series of sonnets, Shakespeare had already attained the highest grade of ideal friendship with him by 1596, for he dedicated his *Venus and Adonis* to him in 1593, and therefore had known him during the three years of Sonnet 104 in 1596. There are indications that the Sonnets were handed about long before 1598. The last line of Sonnet 94, "Lilies that fester smell far worse than weeds" occurs in the play of Edward III., sometimes attributed to Shakespeare. This play was published in 1596, after having been acted in divers places in London. It was, therefore, probably written in 1594 or 1595. The speech in which the line occurs is one in which the Earl of Warwick approves of his daughter, the Countess of Salisbury, for determining to reject the king's shameful suit. It consists of "a spacious field of" eleven "reasons" to show that sin is worse in proportion to the rank or power or knowledge of the sinner. Each reason is condensed into an aphorism, and the form of the whole speech is like one of Sancho Panza's strings of proverbs. It is, therefore, a place where we should least look for originality, and where an author would think least scorn of open plagiarism. It is more probable, then, that this line was quoted from Shakespeare's Sonnets already in 1594 or 1595 known among his private friends, than that it was afterwards adopted by Shakespeare from the play. Yet in 1594 or 1595, when he was only about thirty years of age, he represents himself as a decrepit father, scored and tann'd with age. His indications of time, therefore, seem to be imaginary, and to form a part of the dramatic framework of the poem. Once more, Sonnets

78–86 are devoted to one subject—jealousy of another poet, who is supposed to have supplanted him in his friend's affection. Sonnet 78 declares that his invocations to his friend have been so frequent, and have become so notorious, that "every alien pen" has begun to imitate him, and to dedicate its productions to the same patron. But the poet singles out one competitor, to whom, in comparison with his own "dumbness" and "heavy ignorance," he attributes "learning," "grace," and "majesty" (78)—whom he calls "a worthier pen" (79), "a better spirit," a boat "of tall building and of goodly pride" in comparison to his own "worthless boat," and "saucy bark inferior far to his"—phrases which Fuller seems to have had in mind when he told of Shakespeare and Ben Jonson's contests—(80); and, though in Sonnets 81 and 82 he seems to imply that he was jealous of many others, yet an expression at the end of the latter—"both your poets"—shows that he has only one competitor. This competitor wrote with "strained touches of rhetoric" (82); he buried the life he strove to kindle (83); his "comments of praise" were "charactered with golden quill, and precious phrase by all the Muses filed." He was an "able spirit," writing "in polished form of well-refined pen" (85). His "great verse" was borne along under "proud full sail"; "his spirit was by spirits taught to write above a mortal pitch;" he was aided by "compeers by night"—by an "affable familiar ghost which nightly gulled him with intelligence" (86). These details seem to point more or less distinctly to Marlowe in the character of Dr. Faustus, aided by Mephistopheles. Now Marlowe was killed in 1593. The sonnets of jealousy refer to a period of absence comprising part of the third year of the friendship which they commemorate; and therefore, if we take the indications they contain to be historical, we must suppose that between 1590 and 1592 Shakespeare's Sonnets to some dear friend and patron had gained such notoriety, that all the poets of the day imitated them, and tried to rob him of the monopoly of his friend's favour, and that one of them, Marlowe, succeeded in so doing. This is a piece of history completely unknown to historians, and bred only in the seething brains of the historical commentators on the Sonnets. When Shakespeare published his

Venus and Adonis in 1593, he appeared as a perfectly unknown poet. "If the first heir of my invention," he said, "prove deformed, I shall . . . never after ear so barren a land, for fear it yield me still so bad a harvest." This proves that neither in print nor in manuscript had he become known as a poet (as distinct from a dramatist) before 1593. Hence the indications of the sonnets of jealousy cannot be historical. Each detail may be true of some one, but the whole compilation refers only to an imaginary being.

It is, however, quite clear that Shakespeare had attained a certain dramatic notoriety before 1593. In 1592 Robert Greene had called him "the absolute Johannes Fac-totum, the only Shake-scene in the country," and had characterized him as a daw dressed out in stolen feathers. In 1589 he was already a partner in the Blackfriars Theatre, and was attacked by Nash as a shifting companion, born to the trade of *Noverint*, which he had left to busy himself with the endeavours of art, though he could scarcely Latinize his neck-verse, and had therefore devoted himself to the study of Seneca's ten tragedies, published in English in 1585, whence he stole many good sentences, like "Blood is a beggar," and "whole Hamlets," or "handfuls, of tragical speeches." It is curious to see what use Shakespeare made of the sentence which Nash said he stole. In Sonnet 66 he laments that he has—

> —to behold desert a beggar born,
> And needy nothing trimmed in jollity.

In Sonnet 67 he complains of the degeneracy of his countrymen—

> ——nature bankrupt is,
> Beggar'd of blood to blush through lively veins.

In *King Henry VIII.* Buckingham complains that Wolsey has ruined the nobility, and winds up with the reflection— "A beggar's book outworths a noble's blood." It is curious to see how strong the feeling of family was in Shakespeare, how anxious he was to prove his descent, and the "worship", of his ancestors. With him, a gentleman born is something better than a gentleman made: whatever honour he had for the self-made man, he had a far deeper sympathy for the man who not only deserved but inherited his honours. We find the same feeling in Marlowe's *Edward II.*, but most strongly perhaps in the Catholic productions of the day, such as Andreas Philopater's answer to Elizabeth's Proclamation of November 29, 1591, *Leicester's Commonwealth*, and *Parsons's Memorial for the Reformation of England*, and, curiously enough, in Pius the Fifth's Bull against Elizabeth, which was founded on the representations of English exiles.

More reliance, then, can be placed on the expression of opinions in the Sonnets than on the indication of facts. Yet there are some unquestionable facts plainly alluded to.

> Alas, 'tis true, I have gone here and there,
> And made myself a motley to the view. . . .
> Most true it is, that I have look'd on truth
> Askance and strangely. . . .—(110)
> O, for my sake do you with fortune chide,
> The guilty goddess of my harmful deeds,
> That did not better for my life provide
> Than public means, which public manners breeds.
> Thence comes it that my name receives a brand.—(111)

The references here to his calling of a player cannot be misunderstood. But when we search for the meaning of such Sonnets as 107, 124, 125, which apparently teem with allusions to facts, we can obtain no such certainty. Mr. Gerald Massey has very ingeniously explained Sonnet 107 as a song of triumph for the death of Elizabeth, and the consequent deliverance of Southampton from the Tower. But the Sonnet fits into its place much better when all these supposed allusions are interpreted, not of special facts, but of the general circumstances of love. Not his own fears (of death ending all love) nor the "divining eyes" of the old poets mentioned in Sonnet 106, which had made "ladies dead and lovely knights" into figures of his friend, can set a definite term to his love, which had been supposed to be doomed to come to an end. No— the dying moon has emerged from her eclipse, and the gloomy prognostications of the augurs have proved wrong. Uncertainty is now changed into certainty, and this advanced stage of love promises an endless peace. This balmy time gives a fresh baptism to love; love becomes young again; Death itself is vanquished—because, in spite of death, my rhyme shall live, and shall be my love's monument after the crests and brazen tombs of tyrants are wasted away. Without either affirming or denying Mr. Massey's special interpretation, it is clear that even if the poet had those facts in his mind, he expressed them in general terms, melting them down into a vehicle for the philosophy which it was his principal object to express.

Again, when in Sonnet 124 he declares that his love

> Suffers not in smiling pomp, nor falls
> Under the blow of thralled discontent,
> Whereto the inviting time our fashion calls,

and ends with calling as his witnesses

> The fools of time
> Which die for goodness as they lived for crime,

he speaks as if he and his friend belonged to that "fashion" or faction which was discontented with the Government, and consequently liable to the thraldom of prison life. But he may be speaking only generally, and asserting that true love never suffers by such thraldom. The fools of time may be conspirators—men of Essex's faction, as Mr. Massey thinks; but they may be also politic friendships, which subsist only for selfish ends, and die in an atmosphere of truth and honour, false loves as distinguished from that true one of which he sings in Sonnet 116, "Love's not Time's fool." Again, the opening of Sonnet 125 seems to speak of some special pageant in which the poet "bore the canopy," and laid "great bases for eternity," which at once collapsed—perhaps through the treachery of some spy, for the sonnet concludes with an execration upon the "suborned informer."

But the terms are so general, that whatever guesses they may lead us to make, they can only indicate in what direction we have to look for the facts of Shakespeare's life, but cannot absolutely tell us any of the details. They may serve to illustrate a known history, not to discover the unknown.

Still a curious inspection of the Sonnets will suggest many biographical questions regarding the poet. For instance, Sonnet 14 suggests that he had before his eyes a painting of his friend: after saying that children would be much better likenesses of him than his "painted counterfeit," he goes on,

> So should the lines of life that life repair,
> Which this, Time's pencil, or my pupil pen,
> Neither in inward worth nor outward fair
> Can make you live yourself in eyes of men.

Children being living pictures, the lines with which they are drawn are "lines of life;" and they reproduce the life of the parent better than the painter's pencil can reproduce his "outward fair," or the poet's pen his "inward worth." When he says "this pencil," it looks as if he was the draughtsman. Perhaps, however, if he had been the painter, he would scarcely have called his pencil "Time's pencil;" he may have referred to some master like Giulio Romano, of whom he says in the *Winter's Tale* that "had he himself eternity, and could put breath into his work, he would beguile Nature of her custom, so perfectly is he her ape." Again he speaks of his friend "growing" (18), or being grafted (15) "to Time by eternal lines"—an expression equally applicable to the poet's and to the painter's lines, and concludes—

> So long as men can breathe, or eyes can see,
> So long lives this, and this gives life to thee—

—gives life, while men's breath can recite the poet's, or their eyes see the painter's lines. Again in Sonnet 24 he says—

> Mine eye hath played the painter, and hath stelled
> Thy beauty's form in tables of my heart.

Was Shakespeare a painter, like his friend Burbage, or like Dante, who tells us in his *Vita Nuova* of the angel he drew? Nash gives us to understand that Shakespeare was a man who, when he was twenty-five years old, had already "run through every art and thriven by none."

Such, then, are the biographical uses of Shakespeare's Sonnets. They suggest, without answering, questions on matters of fact. They illustrate the known, without discovering unknown facts. And they furnish a certain key to his inmost sentiments and thoughts on numbers of personal, social, political, artistic, and even religious questions. They are a manual of that philosophy of his which made him, in the estimation of the person who wrote his epitaph,

Socrates ingenio. They ought to be read over and over again, in the light of the philosophy which they avowedly profess. They will be found to illustrate and fall in with the thoughts of the deepest writers on the subject of love. When St. Augustine says "There are in the world but two loves, the love of God extending to the contempt of self, and the love of self extending to the contempt of God," he gives the ultimate expression of the whole scope of the Sonnets. Old writers and new, those who preceded our poet and those who have come after him, if they have chosen his theme, have been forced to run in the same groove; for this love philosophy is a way of stating the realities of human nature; and no one can say that the system which enabled Shakespeare to store, to arrange, to economize, and to exhibit his marvellous knowledge of humanity is a system that has gone out of date, or a philosophy which has been exploded.

www.ingramcontent.com/pod-product-compliance
Lightning Source LLC
Chambersburg PA
CBHW020257090426
42735CB00009B/1117